D0729448

H O S T I N G   T H E
BIRDS

HOSTING THE
BIRDS

How to Attract Birds to Nest in Your Yard

By Jan Mahnken

Illustrations by Kimberlee T. Knauf

A Garden Way Publishing Book

Storey Communications, Inc.
Pownal, Vermont 05261

Front cover photograph by Hal H. Harrison, from Grant Heilman Photography
Cover & Text designed and produced by Nancy Lamb
Color section designed by Cindy McFarland
Production assistant, Kelly Madden
The editors wish to thank René Laubach and Helen Bates for assistance in preparing this book.
Edited by Jill Mason, Deborah Burns, and Anne Lesser

The name Garden Way Publishing has been licensed to Storey Communications, Inc. by Garden Way, Inc.

Copyright © 1989 by Storey Communications, Inc.
First Edition

All rights reserved. No part of this book may be reproduced without written permission from the publisher, except by a reviewer who may quote brief passages or reproduce illustrations in a review with appropriate credits; nor may any part of this book be reproduced, stored in a retrieval system, or transmitted in any form or by any electronic means, mechanical, photocopying, recording, or other, without written permission from the publisher.

Typesetting by Accura Type & Design
Barre, Vermont 05641

Printed in the United States by The Alpine Press
Second Printing, June 1990

Library of Congress Cataloging in Publication Data
Mahnken, Jan.
  Hosting the birds.

  "A Garden Way Publishing book."
  Includes index.
  1. Birds, Attracting of. 2. Birds—Nests.
3. Birds—Habitat. I. Title.
QL676.5.M334 1989   639.9'78   88-45487
ISBN: 0-88266-534-0
ISBN: 0-88266-525-1 (pbk.)

TABLE OF CONTENTS

Preface

For Bud

PREFACE

MORE THAN SIX hundred species of birds nest in North America north of the Mexican border. Since it is impossible (unfortunately) to include all of them in this book I've had to be selective, and some of my decisions about which birds to include have been necessarily arbitrary. I've tried, first of all, to cover all the common garden birds, as well as the more occasional visitors to human environs. In addition, I've included birds that seem of particular interest because they have either beguiling peculiarities or special historical or ecological significance.

I hope you will be pleased with the selection. However, despite my attempt to be reasonable and objective, you may be disappointed that I've not mentioned some favorite of yours. I apologize in advance for the omission and ask your indulgence for what must sometimes be a matter of whimsical choice.

PART I
THE NESTING CYCLE

1 | INTRODUCTION

THEIR CRY SENDS me tearing outside to scan the sky. No matter that the day is cold, that the wind chills me even before I close the door behind me, that the grimy slush in the driveway soaks my sneakers. The first scraggly skein of geese passing northward overhead means that spring is on the way.

The seasonal migration of birds northward signals the visible beginning of their annual nesting cycle. Hormonal changes occurring during the winter eventually send them winging toward summer ranges, there to claim territory, court a mate, and produce offspring. Those biological imperatives attended to and further hormonal changes ending the reproductive urge, survivors young and old prepare for the return flight to winter quarters.

In the chapters that follow, I'll concentrate on the nesting cycles of birds found in and around gardens north of Mexico and south of the subarctic regions. Whether your home is urban, suburban, or rural, you can encourage nesting birds to take up residence. Food, water, and a sheltered nesting site are the essentials: a feeder, a birdbath, and a birdhouse. Gardeners can introduce plants that produce food as well as shelter. Fortuitous geographical features such as a pond or brook, or your own installation of a pool or a fountain, will increase the number of birds that find your garden attractive. Some birds accept nesting boxes (birdhouses) provided by people; even more will accept nesting materials. You can observe birds in all stages of the cycle, provided you are willing to be patient.

No one who enjoys feeding birds needs to be given a reason to do this: it's interesting. If you need more motivation, however, try thinking of bird feeding as a way of repaying a debt to fellow inhabitants of the planet. Having exploited so much of it, we can at least do our best to atone. One way to begin is to learn enough about the nesting requirements of birds to avoid interfering with them, and maybe even help some species to survive.

According to estimates, some twenty-one million people engage in bird watching, a national pastime second in popularity only to gardening. Like gardening, it's an activity you can practice at your own speed. You can be a birder or a Birder, just as you can garden or Garden. No stigma need be attached to lowercase birding. The degree of your participation can vary with your inclination and the time you have to spend. Nor is it necessary to make a big investment in order to enjoy the hobby. All you really need is an interest in birds.

Interest in birds is a worldwide phenomenon. Each summer a friend of mine in Washington, D.C., sends me newspaper clippings reporting the progress of the peregrine falcons that nest annually on a rooftop in downtown Baltimore. On the other side of the world, a female spoonbill duck that nested for five successive years in an artificial pond across from the Imperial Palace in Tokyo attracted even more notice. Each year she led her brood across the busy six-lane highway to spend the summer in the palace's moat. When they thought her crossing was imminent, Tokyo police posted warnings, and the actual event literally stopped traffic, as well as making the newspapers and network television.

Although you can travel widely to observe birds, you don't actually need to leave your own neighborhood. Your immediate area will provide a plethora of birds during the different seasons, according to the habitat each species requires. Look for areas of transition from one kind of plant community to another; they tend to attract more birds of different species than do either of the separate communities. On the fringes of woods, for example, forest-dwelling warblers mingle with chickadees commonly seen at our feeders and in our shrubs. At the edges of swamps shy woodcock compete for earthworms with robins content to nest over our front doors.

Watching the Birds

Up until this century, field ornithology consisted primarily of exploration and classification. Classification usually meant the actual *collection* of nests, eggs, and even birds. It was an effective way to learn about birds, but hardly beneficial to the birds themselves. The modern technique of identifying birds by sight, using their size, shape, flight pattern, and so on as clues, makes a great deal more sense than shooting them does. However, many keen birders collected all three types of specimens, often many sets of the same species. One source reports an individual who had 235 sets of robin's eggs—surely a case of more enthusiasm than good judgment.

Through the conservation movement that began to attract attention around the turn of the century, awareness of the ever-increasing destruction of wildlife made collecting unconscionable to birders and resulted in the activity known as *listing*, in which people keep written records of what they encounter rather than collecting specimens. Today it is against federal law to take nests, eggs, or even the stray feathers of birds if you are not authorized to do so.

Eventually the practice of listing led birders to begin reporting nesting data to the Laboratory of Ornithology at Cornell University, the clearinghouse for such information. Careful, documented observation by amateurs has traditionally been highly useful to ornithologists, and today remains a valuable resource.

In the past, birds were described as being *common, uncommon, occasional*, or *rare* in specified habitats. Such terms were subjective, and their meaning varied according to the experience of the birder reporting or receiving the information. The current practice of *counts* is more appropriate because it provides concrete data less likely to mislead through errors of definition and the vagaries of interpretation. To make these counts, armies of amateur and professional birders gather at a certain time (the Christmas Bird Count attracts a lot of attention) or in a designated area (a flyway, a roosting area, a designated patch of farmland, or near a feeder) and actually count the birds present by species. From these counts, estimates of populations are made.

Now the terms used refer to actual numbers counted. *Abundant* describes birds observed in daily counts of up to fifty and season counts of two hundred and fifty or more. *Common* birds are observed in daily counts of six to fifty and season counts of up to two hundred and fifty. *Uncommon* birds are observed in daily counts of one to five and season counts of five to twenty-five; *rare* birds, five in a season. *Casual* means up to three birds in ten years, and *accidental* is up to three in a lifetime. Approximately eight hundred birds can be identified in North America.

Like all other living organisms, birds are classified in ever-narrowing categories. They belong to the animal kingdom, the vertebrate phylum, the class *Aves*, or birds. There are more birds—over 8,500 living species—than any other vertebrate except fishes. The mountain bluebird is an example of a species; only a subspecies is lower on the ladder of classification. The next larger category in which the mountain bluebird is classified is its genus, *Sialia*. Its family is Muscicapidae and its order Passeriformes, or perching birds.

Altogether there are twenty-seven (a few ornithologists say twenty-nine) orders of birds. Orders are usually worldwide in distribution, but families and groups of genera may be limited to a continent or a zoogeographic region (a large area that has characteristics suitable for them), and genera and species may occur only in certain parts of a continent. An astonishing 85 percent of known species and subspecies of birds are found only in tropical areas, and two-thirds of *them* are found only in the humid parts of the tropics. Considering this, it's not surprising that thirty-two of the forty-four families of birds that exist only in the New World are found exclusively in the tropics. A dozen of the New World families can be found in the United States. They are migratory and winter in the tropics. Moreover, they prefer the humid, eastern part of the United States.

Robin nesting in hanging planter.

Sharing the Planet

Bird numbers fluctuate because of numerous threats to the activities of birds. Human threats have included sport hunting as well as the commercial slaughter of wild birds for meat and feathers; the introduction of bird species that compete with native species; poisonings from lead, pesticides, and other chemicals; and oil spills (auks, for example, will dive when they see one and then surface in its middle).

Environmental changes also affect bird distribution and population. Lowering of the water table tends to displace birds such as the shoveler, the American coot, the common snipe, and the yellow-headed blackbird. Upland sandpipers are disturbed when land is plowed; they prefer grasslands. Although the creation of artificial lakes, especially large ones, will attract water-loving birds, strip-mining is apt to displace birds, even where there is partial reclamation (and often there is none). Stream channelization and asphalt sprawl displace birds, although soil conservation programs and the protection of woodlands in state and national parks and forests help to maintain existing populations.

Structures such as television towers, skyscrapers, and even windows take an annual toll. Recreational activities such as swimming, sunning, and driving vehicles in nesting and feeding areas drive birds away. The draining of wetlands and competition from fisheries endanger the food sources of some birds. There is speculation that human-induced climate changes alter migration patterns. Certain other weather-related problems, not attributable to people, include the unreliability of the food supply, the effect of temperature and precipitation on breeding, the disturbance of flight by heavy winds, and the destruction of birds by storms.

Although many human activities have been injurious to birds, it is worth mentioning that certain birds cause problems for human beings, who are also part of the ecological scheme. Mute swans may eat, trample, or foul the grass in grazing pastures, and Canada geese make serious inroads on grain crops in some areas. Starlings wreak havoc in orchards. Many farmers in England consider the wood pigeon a serious agricultural pest and the bullfinch a horticultural pest. Linnets attack strawberries and other soft fruits; tits damage roses; and jays savage the beans. In North America, fecal deposits under the winter roosts of such birds as starlings and red-winged blackbirds can kill trees. (As many as twenty or thirty *million* red-winged blackbirds may inhabit a single roost in the southern states.) The herring gull can even damage airplanes, shattering windshields and jamming turbine blades. At the same time, of course, birds provide such invaluable services as eating insects and distributing seeds and pollen—not to mention the aesthetic pleasures they offer.

Although most birds are specialized, some are highly adaptable, demonstrating an ability to benefit from human activities as we benefit from theirs. Starlings, house sparrows, and pigeons, introduced to North America by human beings, have adapted so well that many people now consider them nuisances. Some highly attractive native species have also proved adaptable. Peregrine falcons nest in cities to feed on the introduced pigeons. Robins, swallows, barn-owls, crows, and ospreys have all profited from the presence of humans who have provided structures that these birds use and have cleared land, thus making available more habitats of the sort these species require. Certain other machine-made changes to the environment, such as reservoirs and gravel pits, have been helpful to species common to similar natural features. And, as previously mentioned, many species make good use of synthetic nests and nesting materials provided by human beings.

Does it all balance out? That's a question we must address, if only for selfish reasons. Quite aside from all the other reasons for an interest in birds, there's the old canary-in-the-mine business. Just as miners gauged their safety by the condition of their caged birds, so might we. As the authors of *Kentucky Birds: A Finding Guide* so aptly put it, "In the collapse of certain indicator species we anticipate our own peril." When birds are endangered, humans may be in trouble, too.

2 | TERRITORY

Talking about territory in reference to birds gets confusing unless we define some terms at the outset. First of all, *habitat* and *range* should be distinguished from *territory*. *Habitat* is the kind of landscape a particular species needs. *Range* is that wide geographical area in which a species can be found. Breeding range includes any place where nests of the species are found, its seasonal distribution. Wintering range refers to any area in which the species is found in winter.

There are two kinds of *territory*. One is the actual amount of land a pair of birds needs in order to assure themselves and their offspring an adequate food supply. This amount varies widely. For example, the density of breeding red-eyed vireos may vary from ten territorial males in one hundred acres of open slash land to one hundred territorial males in one hundred acres of virgin hardwood deciduous forest. There must be enough food to feed both the parents and the young. A wren family might subsist in a single garden, but an eagle needs a square mile of land and a kingfisher a linear mile of open water. The size of the territory depends not only on the food supply in a particular area, but also on the duties of the nest. Incubating the eggs and caring for the young occupy so much time that the birds must minimize the area in which they search for food.

The other kind of territory is that which the male defends against other males of his own species. Studies of the red-eyed vireo have shown that this, too, varies, from 0.3 acre

Cattle egrets.

to 2.4 acres in his case, again depending apparently on the relative abundance of food within the territory. Many males defend only a smallish territory in the immediate vicinity of the nest, and the birds use communal feeding grounds. Colonial birds (birds that nest in groups) such as swallows and gulls defend only the territory they can reach while sitting on the nest. The purple martin defends only the nest cavity itself.

Selection of a territory assures the proper distribution of a species. Familiarity with a given area enables the bird to be self-sufficient and to reserve for its own use the specialized nest site it requires, as well as to avoid predators and to find food and nesting material more easily. This efficiency is necessary if the birds are to concentrate on the job of raising their young. Moreover, using a restricted area helps establish a sexual bond between the parents.

Generally speaking, the territory is selected by the male. In those cases where mating occurs before migration, the pair may choose the nesting territory together. Because the male defends his territory, allowing no other males within it, the sexual bond between male and female is necessarily strengthened once the pairing has been accomplished. Other birds of their species are excluded, and...out of sight, out of mind.

Having selected a territory, birds defend it against others of their own species. Generally, it is the males who assume much of the defense. One of the common ways of defending territory is by singing. By moving from perch to perch around the perimeter of his territory, the bird signals to others of his species that his turf is off-limits to them.

Getting Down to Cases

Territorial behavior varies widely from species to species, so it's important to mention particulars of individual species.

Cattle egrets have expanded their range dramatically since they first appeared in the southern United States a couple of decades ago; they can now be found as breeding birds as far north as Vermont and New Hampshire and as far west as Minnesota. These colonial birds are often found in the company of herons, though they are less aquatic. They defend a territory of several yards around their nests until incubation begins, at which time they restrict their defense to the nest itself. However, each bird defends a feeding territory as well, often around a particular domestic animal.

A pair of mallards typically needs an eighth to a quarter of an acre of feeding territory. The male defends only a small area of water and reeds, not including the nest, for ten to fourteen days until incubation begins.

Canada geese defend an area of a quarter-acre to an acre until the time of hatching. A Canada goose defending his territory is not to be taken lightly. As a mild threat, he lowers his head at his opponent and hisses. If intending to attack, the male calls *ahonk* (the female's version is simply *honk*) and rapidly raises and lowers his head. Very aggressive behavior preceding an attack consists of waving his head and neck back and forth; interestingly enough, such behavior is also part of the greeting behavior of mates.

American kestrels claim a territory of 250 acres and defend it from March until June. On the other hand, the colonial herring gull defends an area of only thirty to fifty yards in diameter, chasing or fighting intruders at its boundaries. Newly mated pairs patrol the periphery.

The rock dove defends an even smaller territory, only the immediate vicinity of the nest itself. During the breeding cycle, the male will bow at opponents and strike at them with outstretched wing. The male Inca dove defends a cleared area with trees nearby, from 30 x 50 to 70 x 100 yards, after courtship and before the laying of eggs. At other times, Inca doves are highly social.

Chimney swifts defend no territory whatever. The rufous hummingbird, however, is the most aggressive of a highly aggressive family. Both sexes defend territories, a practice common to all hummingbirds: the female defends the nest area, the male the feeding territory.

Northern flickers range throughout an area of half a square mile but defend only the nest area, displaying head bobbing, a frozen pose, and drumming (beating a tattoo with their beaks on a resonant branch). The hairy woodpecker defends an area of a quarter-acre around the nest site by drumming, chasing, and perching, but he ranges throughout a larger area. Oddly enough, his smaller relative, the downy woodpecker, defends an area of about four acres.

The eastern kingbird, an aggressive defender of his half-acre, will attack crows, hawks, or owls even a hundred feet over his territory. He also proclaims his property by what is called the *tumble-flight*, in which he flies very high, glides down in stages, and then tumbles through the air.

Tree swallows defend the immediate area of their nests by chasing intruders. Crows, too, defend only the immediate area of the nest; social creatures, they use huge communal roosts. Although blue jays have ill-defined territories, they are aggressive toward interlopers, especially squirrels and cats. Their usual attack is dive bombing. The territory of the scrub jay consists of a single scrub oak.

Black-capped and Carolina chickadees (which are hard to tell apart and which occasionally hybridize where their ranges overlap) have a feeding territory, from August to February, of about twelve to twenty acres, which is defined by the flock using it. Except in the northern portions of their range, where chickadees tend to be migratory, these small resident flocks consist of the same birds throughout the year. Within the flock there is a dominance hierarchy. A pair found around a feeding station in summer is very likely the dominant pair of the winter flock. Birds feeding together may be "friends" or mates. Chickadees breed, however, in isolated pairs. From March to July, the *fee-bee* song of the male announces a breeding territory of a half-acre to about ten acres, which he defends aggressively with short chases of rivals and occasional fights.

White-breasted nuthatches claim a territory of twenty-five to fifty acres, but the house wren needs only a half to three-quarters of an acre. Bewick's wren claims an area of fifty to one hundred yards before the house wren arrives on the scene.

Mockingbirds use a feeding territory of about twelve acres and a breeding territory of one or two acres. The male sings, chases, dive bombs, and displays drooped wings and a loose tail in defense of the breeding territory. Mockingbirds are unusual in that they have fall territory battles to protect their food supply; however, they usually remain on their summer territory in winter. Mockingbirds, by the way, do not seem to mimic the sounds of other birds, or other sounds, if they're busy raising a family or defending territory. Mocking seems to have the status of a hobby for birds not otherwise employed.

California thrashers are highly aggressive in defending the area near the nest site in their territory of five to ten acres. They have been known to attack human intruders. Catbirds claim a smaller territory, and the pair together defends it by song, chases, the body fluff, and the raised wing. The male defends against birds, and the female joins in defense against other intruders. A density of eighty pairs of catbirds per one hundred acres has been reported; the typical area for a pair is one to three acres.

Rock dove defends vicinity of its nest.

Robins use a territory of a third-acre to an acre, but territories often overlap, giving rise to chases and fights. The wood thrush defends a fifth-acre to two acres. Starlings, usually social, defend the nest area through crowing, bill-wipes, fluffing, wing-flicks, and sidling.

Red-eyed vireos defend one to two acres of forest habitat through song, chases, tail-fanning, and crest-erecting. Yellow warblers may need up to twenty acres, but in a favorable habitat sixty-eight pairs have been found in a square mile. Common yellowthroats defend from a half-acre to two acres by singing from exposed perches, vocal duels, chases, short flights around the boundaries, wing-flicks, and song-flights. The latter consist of flying at an angle for twenty-five to one hundred feet, giving sharp call notes. These birds defend until the nestling stage (after the eggs have hatched) and then again for the second brood.

House sparrows remain sociable even during nesting; it is not unusual to find four or five nests in close proximity in a small tree. They defend only the nest itself, with the *churr* call and head extended forward. Red-winged blackbirds defend an eighth- to a quarter-acre, always adjacent to other red-winged blackbird territories, by song, bill-tilt, song-flight, and tail-flick. They will actually strike intruders, including humans, banding together for the purpose.

Tricolored blackbirds protect a territory of only six square feet. Their nest sites are always colonial and may contain anywhere from fifty to thousands of nests. In their colonies, common grackles defend four to eight square yards at the nest site by perch-taking. Northern (Baltimore) orioles give six or seven loud whistles in defense of territory; orchard orioles do virtually nothing and are even willing to share a tree with another pair.

Song sparrows defend their half- to one-and-a-half-acre territories by singing from perches and puffing out their feathers; the defense ceases during the late summer. The American goldfinch defends a similar territory by chases and circular flights.

As many as fifty-two pairs of indigo buntings have been reported on one hundred acres of favorable habitat in Maryland. Defense consists of the male singing from a perch; it ceases with the August molt.

The only constant in territory seems to be the area around the nest site defended by a particular species. Other than that, density varies with the suitability of the habitat and its productivity in any given year, factors which themselves vary widely.

Some experts disparage the "intelligence" of birds, contending that birds can distinguish sex only through behavior and can't even determine whether or not another bird is alive. Jays will mob a stuffed owl....

3 | COURTSHIP

My DEAREST FRIEND has a family of house sparrows living in a birdhouse attached to a tree near her kitchen window. House sparrows are not exclusively cavity-nesters; had more luxurious quarters not been available, they would have been entirely happy to nest in the wisteria vine beneath the window. They were not the species she had hoped to attract, but once they laid claim to the property, Winnie didn't discourage them. Nothing is busier than a busy house sparrow, and that goes far in removing any stigma attached to interest in their behavior. Yes, they're common as dirt; still, their homebody attitudes endear them to all of us devoted to family life, whether in practice or theory. House sparrows are among the few birds we observe that use their nests year round as residences. Moreover, they have persistent family arrangements, are sedentary rather than migratory, and tolerate—encourage is more like it—close observation on a daily basis.

Because of their proximity, Winnie is privy to the considerable domestic activity of the sparrows. They nested first in mid-April and by July they were raising a second brood and entertaining an entire family of humans with what seemed to be inordinate quantities of generalized bickering and squabbling. Since not all of us have the leisure or the inclination to spend time in blinds observing the activities of more exotic birds, it's pleasant to be able to watch birds close to home. Winnie's observations of the inelegant sparrows enlarged her interest in birds generally.

Propagating the Species

Much of what we know about reproduction in birds stems from the pioneering work of Professor William Rowan at the University of Alberta in the 1930s. He studied photoperiodism (the effects of differing periods of light) in birds. Working with crows and juncos, he discovered that artificially increasing the length of periods of light in fall and winter caused the birds' sex organs to emerge from the resting state and enlarge. This information tells us only about reproductive behavior in birds of the temperate zone, however, where day length varies with the season. Tropical birds may breed at any time of the year. In Africa and Australia rainfall patterns affect nesting, whatever the time of year.

The only constant seems to be that, wherever the birds, there is always a cycle of rest, which may last several months. During this "refractory" period, the reproductive organs don't respond to any stimulus. Following it, however, birds can become sexually responsive to factors other than light. Warmth, rainfall, food, and the presence of mates and nest sites also stimulate the sex organs. Cold, aridity, as well as a lack of food, nest sites, and social stimulation retard their enlargement.

Males are ready to mate before females, and they proceed to engage in courtship displays. Their earlier readiness may explain the pronounced dimorphism (difference between the sexes) in some birds. This dimorphism may be seen not only in plumage (such as that of grosbeaks) but also in behaviors. Sage grouse, for example, gather in arenas every morning for a period of weeks. While the females watch from the sidelines, the males fight until a hierarchy is formed. The dominant male eventually mates with most of the females, though males lower on the scale sometimes mate with females while the dominant bird is occupied. In the courtship of waxwings, males offer berries to females in much the same manner and spirit that people might offer chocolates. Food offerings help species in which males and females look alike to distinguish the sexes. Food accepted from a male tern in the properly submissive way indicates he has found a female; if his accompanying pecks provoke a beak-grappling contest, he's guessed wrong.

Other displays in male birds include strange postures, loud vocalizations, and manipulation of sacs on the throat or feathers of the crest, ruff, or tail. Visual displays can resemble dances and some involve what ornithologists call nonvocal songs—drumming, or the whirring of wings. (In addition to those displays intended to attract females are defensive displays, threats against other males of the species in defending territory; and distraction behaviors, simulating injury or sickness, by which males and females try to lure enemies away from the nest.)

Differences in plumage in males and females of the same species include patterns on wings or tail and the colors of the feet or bill. Brilliantly colored songbirds engage in fewer extravagant courtship displays than do the less colorful; it is thought that the bright plumage is sufficient to attract the female. (There are exceptions, of course, such as the peacock, which engages in elaborate displays despite his brilliant plumage.) Spring plumage is nuptial plumage, whether the bird is breeding or not. Although the prenuptial molt may be only a partial one, the eventual breaking off of the neutral feather tips of winter plumage reveals the brighter colors. (You may have noticed how speckled the starlings look throughout the winter and how glossy they become in spring. The speckles are merely colors at the tips of the feather.)

An interesting feature of plumage is that in species in which the sexes look alike, the male and female usually share equally in nest building, incubation, and care of the young. Barn and tree swallows are examples. Wrens, chickadees—even the raucous jays—share domestic chores. On the other hand, where is the male red-winged blackbird, rufous hummingbird, or pheasant when his mate is busy with nest duties? For that matter, what rooster would be caught dead in a nest?

Most birds are monogamous for at least one nesting season, and nonmigratory birds are likely to remain mated for a year or longer. Birds will usually mate again if the partner dies; mortality is high during the nesting season, but there is always a floating population of unmated birds. When one sex greatly outnumbers another, homosexual pairing sometimes occurs, especially among captive birds. Some few species change mates between broods. In crowded colonies of red-winged blackbirds, a male may find it difficult to defend his territory against the great numbers of other males. Sometimes a female red-wing mates with more than one male.

The pairing period usually starts at the end of the spring migration. (Some large birds that don't breed until they are two or three years old spend all of their first year in their winter quarters.) Generally, the male begins to demonstrate his range of courtship displays as soon as a female arrives on an established territory. The female is usually unreceptive to copulation at first; the displays eventually stimulate her to accept it.

Displays enable the sexes to attract each other even though they are rivals for food. The male's sexual displays attract females and repulse other males. These displays continue after copulation to maintain the pair bonds that ensure proper care of the young. Some sexual displays, such as male nest building or courtship feeding, are symbolic. The begging display—usually the gaping and the pecking of juveniles—is sometimes also a courtship display; sexual pursuit often accompanies it. Aquatic birds pursue on water; others pursue in the air or on the ground. A few birds, such as hummingbirds and birds of prey, court exclusively on the wing. During the period of active sexual display, males and some females of certain species, such as cardinals and robins, become so aggressive that they fight their own reflections in water or in a hubcap.

Sexual displays usually coincide with arrival at the breeding site. The pair forms and builds the nest, mating occurs, eggs are laid and incubated. The eggs hatch, the young are raised, and then the family breaks up. Breeding cycles are timed so that the fledglings leave the nest when the climate is most favorable and food most plentiful. In the northeastern United States, for example, returning birds rest and then lay eggs in May, but wanderers like cedar waxwings and permanent residents like American goldfinches lay in summer and feed their young on berries and weed seeds, not insects. Since they're in no hurry to get anywhere on schedule, they can afford an apparently leisurely approach.

Getting Down to Cases

Enough generalities. Let's begin with examples of monogamous aquatic birds. Trumpeter swans, which mate for life, pair even before they are sexually mature. During courtship they engage in a mutual display in the water. Facing each other, with wings half-spread, they rise out of the water and then return to it, swimming in circles. Canada geese also pair for life before sexual maturity and, in addition, behave as if they grieve the loss of a partner. In courtship they stand side by side, honk, and curve their necks. It doesn't sound like much, but it satisfies the geese.

Ducks are monogamous, but the females have the job of rearing the young. The males are frequently almost gaudy in their nuptial plumage. Ruddy ducks, for example, wear rusty red plumage, black caps, and blue bills for courtship. Males chase a female on water, and she chooses the one she wants. Mallards engage in group displays before forming pairs, courtship beginning in the fall and continuing until spring. Males shake both heads and tails, arch their necks with heads pointing to the water, and whistle. Both males and females engage in mock preening. Immediately preceding copulation pairs face each other, bobbing their heads. Forced copulation is common among mallards during both incubation and fledgling care.

Grouse exhibit interesting courtship behavior. Inflatable air sacs on their necks increase the resonance of their calls during courtship; these calls are referred to as *booming*. On the prairie chicken the sacs are bright orange, with erectile black feathers above them. At their *booming grounds* (the site they select as a courting arena) as many as fifty cocks may be seen together annually, heads and necks thrust forward, with inflated air sacs, drooping wings, and raised tails. After booming, they stamp their feet, turn, and run in circles. Mating occurs on the spot after the ceremonial dances. Males are polygamous; the female departs the booming grounds and goes about her matronly duties alone. Sharp-tailed grouse engage in a similar performance, but the ruffed grouse makes his drumming sound with his wings.

Whooping cranes, which share the responsibilities of bringing up their young, share also in their courtship display. The male approaches the female and bows. After that, both birds display, with marvelously synchronized flaps, steps, and stances, at the end of which the male may leap completely over the female. Her opinion of this bizarre demonstration is apparently favorable. North American laughing gulls have a peculiar problem, though not a unique one. Because the sexes look alike, a male charges another gull to find out its sex; another male invariably countercharges. If the charged gull does not return the action, the male turns and faces in the opposite direction. Both gulls turn their heads from side to side, and then the female initiates a symbolic food-begging ritual. Eventually she crouches to indicate receptivity to copulation.

Herring gulls engage in mate feeding and head tossing. After forming a pair, the male regurgitates food for the female. Perhaps ritual feeding of the female of various species developed from the female's increased caloric needs at breeding time.

Northern harriers engage in spectacular nuptial flights. The male dives repeatedly from a height of about 60 feet (occasionally from as high as 500 feet) to within 10 feet of the ground,

In *The Courtship of Birds*, Hilda Simon reports a peacock that displayed only to giant tortoises, with which it grew up, and a jackdaw that offered food only to the naturalist who raised it. Both birds were *imprinted*, a phenomenon familiar to anyone who has raised a newly hatched gosling where no adult geese were present, or an infant mammal, for that matter. The babies assume that the first thing they see is a parent. Unless the impression is corrected by association with others of their species, they persist in the faulty conclusion and demonstrate abnormal behaviors.

then climbs and repeats the performance, usually about twenty-five times. The record observed is seventy-one uninterrupted dives and swoops. Male American kestrels dive from the heights and swoop upward over the nesting area. Kestrels court for about six weeks, copulating as often as fifteen times a day, then separating and preening.

Courtship among doves—common symbols of peace and love—follows the furious battles of the males, who beat one another with their wings. Among Inca doves, the older birds pair before the younger ones do. Both males and females engage in much head bobbing, cooing, and mutual preening; the males add vertical tail-fanning to their performance. Both rock doves and mourning doves mate for life. With puffed feathers and trembly wings, the males strut, bow their heads, and coo. Male mourning doves perform the "tower dance," in which they fly to a height of about 30 feet and flutter, descend a little and flutter again, and so on. Sometimes the male circles above his mate, his tail fanned. The male spotted dove, introduced to the Los Angeles area from Southeast Asia, rises 100 feet from a high perch and then plummets earthward in spirals.

The group flights, trio flights, and V-gliding (groups of birds gliding in V-formation) of chimney swifts are probably part of their courtship rituals. They mate in flight and at the nest site. The male Allen's hummingbird flies to an altitude of about 75 feet and then dives, swoops upward, and flies back and forth rapidly in a semicircular arc, squealing. At the top of the arc he spreads his tail, shakes his body, and dives again. He repeats this performance several times and then rises to 75 feet again and starts over.

The courtship flight of Anna's hummingbird is similar, but the ruby-throated hummingbird perches and waits for the female and then commences a pendulum-like courtship flight of from 3 to 40 feet, lasting anywhere from two to twenty minutes. Sometimes he rises high, dives, faces the female, and spreads wings and tail before rising again. In another ceremony, the male faces the nest and makes a sideways flight of about 25 feet east to west and then back again, stopping about every 3 feet to hover and hum. Males and females perform one characteristic courtship flight together. Starting about 2 feet apart, they fly up and down at a range of 10 feet for two or three minutes at a time in opposite directions, so that when the male is at the top of the flight, the female is at the bottom, and vice versa.

It's not surprising that the swifts and hummers conduct their courtship in the air; their feet are very weak, not at all appropriate for the perching and walking common to many orders. Despite all their complicated courtship activity, once they mate the male disappears completely, leaving all the household chores to the female.

Courtship among flickers is simple but a little peculiar, consisting largely of head-bobbing and a fluttering flight. The wild part is that two females may court one male (he's the one with the black mustache, obviously). Male hairy woodpeckers drum, "still-pose" (just what it sounds like), and make fluttering flights. Their diminutive look-alikes, the downy woodpeckers, merely flap from tree to tree and sail in a deep loop.

The eastern kingbird is well known for being an aggressive bird, and even in courtship the male seems hostile at first, as if he were just as willing to drive the female away from his territory as entice her to share it. The wing flutter is characteristic of his courtship. Tree swallows engage in flutter flight, bowing, and billing.

The courtship of blue jays is surprisingly inconspicuous and may consist primarily of bobbing and mate feeding. It is not unusual to see a flock of males chasing a single female at breeding time. Such chasing is noisy, but what else would you expect from jays? The numbers involved gradually diminish until a single pair remains—silent. Such chases may involve first-time breeders.

Not much is known of the courtship of Clark's nutcracker, which is assumed to be even quieter than that of the jays. Courtship among their kin, the crows, begins with fighting in the flock. Considering their usual behavior, that isn't surprising. But can you believe that mated crows bill like doves? During courtship they perch on a limb together. The male walks toward the female, bows, ruffles his feathers, and spreads his wings and tail. He lifts his head up and then lowers it. It's all very courtly, and his lady is impressed.

Male robin attacking hub-cap on car.

Courtship behavior of the tufted titmouse is unknown, which we can count as one blow for privacy. Some believe it is ritual feeding of the female and wing fluttering of both male and female. I suspect that conjecture is based on the known behavior of some of their relatives, such as the chickadees. We know that wing fluttering is the principal courtship behavior of black-capped chickadees, occurring from March through June, after the breakup of the winter flocks. The pair bill-touches and feeds each other. Rather more spectacularly, boreal chickadees mate-feed in midair, the female fluttering her wings and ruffling her feathers.

White-breasted nuthatches are examples of birds that mate for life rather than for the breeding season. The male in courtship bows, sings, and pretends to intimidate the female. Somewhat more complicated is the ritual of the male red-breasted nuthatch, which struts before the female, flirting his wings and tail and bowing. As an added fillip, he flies in an ellipse 100 feet long above the tops of the pines.

Once a male house wren has found a suitable territory, he begins singing to defend his domain and attract a female. He fills the houses in his territory with sticks; in due time a female appears and begins to inspect nesting sites while he makes trembling movements of wings and tail and performs a flutter flight. The male winter wren is busy, too. He actually builds several nests and shows them to the female for her approval. She chooses what she thinks is the best of the lot. The male, apparently unwilling to let his labors go in vain, shows the remaining nests to a second female—and gets a second mate.

Among the Mimidae, the brown thrasher struts and trails his tail to win a mate, and seeks a new one for the second brood. Male catbirds display spread wings and tail. They also pursue the female in flight, then bow, raising their plumage, and strut.

The mockingbird picks out an elevated perch from which to sing. From the perch, he jumps and somersaults. After chasing a female, the male performs a loop-flight. Once the female is attracted, they engage in a "dance," facing each other on the ground about a foot apart and hopping from side to side, either in unison or alternately. The male also stretches his wings, moves his spread tail up and down, and coos. He may pick up a twig and run back and forth with it. Maybe that's his promise of helping with the nest building.

Red-eyed vireo males chase females, too, but the rest of their show is merely the tail-fan and sway. On the other hand, male robins become quite aggressive after their flocks break up and fight each other (or their reflection) as if they were gamecocks. They lower their heads and lift their tails, crouching, to attract a female; they are normally, but not necessarily,

Great physical energy, excitement, curiosity, and fear of predators are characteristic during all seasons, but during courtship anger appears in the repertoire of behaviors.

monogamous. Their relatives, the wood thrushes, confine their efforts to chasing females very fast through the forest.

Starlings wing-wave and chase in courtship and save the interesting stuff for nest building, where it counts. Common yellowthroats fly around in pairs and the female wing-quivers to show acceptance of a male—pretty tame stuff compared to some other species. Male house sparrows, however, become as quarrelsome as robins at mating time. They wing-stretch and wing-quiver, and bob in a crouch. The female opens her bill and lunges at the male, looking rather as if she intended him serious bodily harm. He, evidently, knows better.

Polygamy and polyandry are more common to game birds than to songbirds, but there are exceptions. Male red-winged blackbirds average three mates each. They perform song-flights, crouch, and chase their chosen females, with each of whom they spend about three weeks. Common grackles approach females with heads down, bills tilted, fanning wings and tail and ruffling the feathers of neck and back. The female wing-quivers in acceptance. The male leaves her while she's incubating the eggs and finds another mate, which is probably just fine for the species but seems a trifle hard on the female.

Monogamous northern (Baltimore) orioles droop their wings and tails, fan them, bowing their heads and whistling, then flutter in the air. Orchard orioles simplify the show, simply bowing before the female and singing vigorously. Maybe they're too frazzled with the whole idea of getting the cycle finished up by July, when they migrate south, to waste time on preliminaries.

If you're out in the woods in springtime and think you hear an army of moose approaching, it may be only a rufous-sided towhee chasing a female he fancies. The amount of racket towhees can make as they go about their activities is impressive. In courtship, both males and females rapidly open and close their wings and tails in display.

Little is known about the courtship of the western tanager, but it may include food-offering. Song sparrows tend to be more visible than towhees; they're aggressive and chase other males as well as females, one assumes with different intentions.

Among birds you're likely to observe close to home is the cardinal; the male chases a female and fights other males and swoops and dives. With luck and the right location you might glimpse the gorgeous painted bunting when he struts and spreads his wings and tail. Painted buntings are so pugnacious toward other males that sometimes their fights are fatal.

Later in the season, be on the lookout for an American goldfinch chasing a female. Chances are good—sometimes the pursuit lasts for as long as twenty minutes, in a flat flight. The house finch circles the female with short strutting hops, droops wings, raises the feathers of crown and crest.

I always eagerly await the arrival of the rose-breasted grosbeaks in spring; they're among my favorites because they're extraordinarily beautiful, better even than the orioles. The males fight. They also sing and hover in the air around the female during courtship.

4 | BIRD SONG

IN 1650 ATHANASIUS KIRCHER published a book that described some bird songs in musical notation, but what is considered scientific study of bird song didn't get underway until the twentieth century. Eliot Howard, an English ornithologist, is credited with laying the foundations for such study at the beginning of the century.

In 1904, F. Schuyler Mathews published his *Field Book of Wild Birds and Their Music*, a famous source which uses normal musical scales to illustrate bird song. It has long been out of print, but many libraries have copies. It is very complete—though a little weird in its subjectivity. In his preface Mathews says, "He [the bird] can not sustain a melody of any considerable length, nor can he conform to our conventional ideas of metre, but he can keep time perfectly, and a knowledge of his rhythmic methods is, I believe, the strongest factor in his identification by the ear!"

In 1935 Aretas A. Saunders published *Guide to Bird Songs*, which introduced various formulas for identification and phonetic syllabification; it is still considered helpful. The development of electronic sound recording and spectographs has made possible an objective study of bird song, which is part of a whole complex of integrated behavior. Even though individual songs may vary widely, characteristics are usually present that make possible the identification of the species.

Bird song is part of the courtship displays. Like the nonvocal songs that often accompany them, such as drumming or the whirring of wings, courtship displays require both specialized organs and a certain development of the brain. So does vocal *song*, which demands more learning (including imitation) than the *calls* of birds. The calls are often a single sound, such as squawking, peeping, or screaming. Even if the call is repeated, it's likely to lack variation. Calls serve a variety of purposes, however, including scolding; warning; begging; indicating alarm, anger, or a location; or sending a summons.

Songs consist of a series of notes in a more or less discernible pattern. They tend to be more leisurely, more relaxed, and they first occur as youthful play. They are relatively short because of the limited attention spans of birds. Females don't usually sing as much as males do, but they are more likely to sing in the tropics than in temperate zones. A female chickadee has only the *fee-bee* song; on the other hand, female cardinals sing as well as their mates. Singing in males is closely correlated with the presence of male hormones and is at its loudest during the breeding season.

Although bird song is part of the courtship performance, it is used for more than announcing a claim to territory or attracting a mate. Through their songs birds can identify not only their own species, but individuals of their species. That can be very important. Birds may produce, say, twenty eggs in a lifetime and only just manage to replace themselves, which is surely indicative of the perilous lives they lead. They must be able to tell who's who, as well as to recognize the calls that signal distress, hunger, and alarm. Visual signals aren't enough. Not only are birds of the same species similar to one another, but also many females of *different* species strongly resemble each other. Examples include multitudes of sparrows, purple and house finches, dickcissels, siskins, pipits, and longspurs. No one has yet decided whether bird song is music or language, poetry or prose, but it must be distinctive at a distance in order to serve its purposes.

Though prenuptial singing is the richest, songs accompany nest building, incubation, tending the young, the departure of the young, roosting, autumn, migration, and winter. Through their vocalizations, birds proclaim territory, issue mating invitations and invitations to the nest, request relief from the nest, maintain and strengthen a sexual bond, and abet flock formation.

On the theory that animals enjoy their essential activities, some students of bird song believe that though a correlation between need and skill exists, the skillful sing even if the need is not pressing, and with more frequency and variation than seems required. They point out that just as human music has its purposes—such as serving as stimulation in war, love, and magic—so, too, birds sing to express feelings. No one would argue that birds are as musically sophisticated as human beings are, but however primitive their song is, it persists when no actual need can be demonstrated.

Some experts not opposed to ruminating on philosophical themes believe bird song is sometimes used as an emotional release, described either as an excess of energy or an outpouring of sheer joy and called *ecstasy song*. Such song is produced randomly and is sometimes accompanied by the so-called *ecstasy flight*. Believing that this activity is motivated by a hope of harmony and escape from discord and boredom will not be easy for everyone to do, but I'm willing to entertain the idea. Even if you subscribe to the principle of parsimony in nature—that is, that nothing is wasted—that need not rule out the possibility of aesthetic feeling. (I'm talking about aesthetic *feeling*, not aesthetic thought.)

Some attempt has been made to quantify certain aspects of bird song to find out how the annual amount of song correlates with the degree of need, with development, or with the distribution of accomplished singers in various taxonomic groups. Ornithologists study simple

Sometimes bird song is divided into primary and secondary song. Under the primary song heading comes male territorial song to repel other males and attract females; signals used to coordinate activities, especially with those of the mate; emotional song (reason unknown); and female song, which is less common in North America than in other parts of the world. Secondary song includes whisper song, which is territorial song without territorial implications (that is, it is not intended to exclude rival birds or even be heard by them) and is produced by either sex at any time; and subsong, which is unlike territorial song and is produced mostly by juveniles. Subsong may be compared to the play of young animals; it is a kind of practicing by the immature birds.

repetition, repetition with variations, the repertoire of repeated songs, that repertoire plus its variations, variable sequences, and medley sequences. We know that the amount and the quality of singing are positively correlated.

Imitation is common among songbirds, and we suspect that imitation signifies interest in sounds as such. Birds in a given region develop what might be called dialects, just as people do. Bird dialects always have this geographical basis despite a hereditary predisposition to certain basic types of utterance. Isolation of a group of, say, chickadees, from others of their species, promotes dialect formation. Call notes are more constant than songs because less imitation (learning) is involved. "Accents" show up better in the learned songs than in innate calls.

In her book, *Bird Songs*, Norma Stillwell tells how she and her husband took to the road and began taping bird songs as a more or less full-time activity after they retired. In travels from their base in Texas, they discovered a wide variation in song, depending on where the birds lived. (They also experimented with the aesthetic dimensions of bird songs by having a friend recite Whitman's "Out of the Cradle Endlessly Rocking" to the recorded song of a mockingbird.) Gradually they got more and more sophisticated equipment, learning the best techniques for using it as they went along, and continued traveling during the "song season," going south in March and following the birds until about early July. They recorded three volumes of "Bird Songs of Dooryard, Field and Forest," which have been widely distributed.

Song sparrow singing.

Some of the songs that birds create are unique to the individual, even though the song developed initially through mimicry. We are all aware of the ability of mockingbirds to mimic bird songs, as well as other sounds. It is actually possible to learn the songs of other species by listening to mockingbird imitations. Other members of the Mimidae family may sound much like the mockingbird, but they can identify their own species fairly easily. Catbirds sing a phrase only once; thrashers repeat it; and mockingbirds repeat it several times. It is estimated that a thrasher is capable of uttering a thousand recognizably different songs. A number of birds can even be taught to "talk," although this is possible only with captive birds—they apparently will not do it in the wild. Maybe captives learn to talk as a form of social adaptation—to get the attention they need.

The songs humans enjoy most tend to be the territorial songs of birds that are visually rather inconspicuous—precisely the birds that have the greatest need of distinctive songs, since they otherwise blend into their surroundings so well that they're hard to detect even by others of their own species. Each species usually has two or more distinct types of song, which may have regional variations. Cardinals have two dozen or more, and Aretas Saunders noted 884 variations in song sparrow songs.

The best singers are perching birds, especially the thrushes (Muscicapidae), mimic thrushes (Mimidae), and wrens (Troglodytidae). Families, of course, differ ecologically and presumably in their ancestry—and that correlates with the degree of their song development. (If song helps assure success in breeding, through evolution birds eventually develop the necessary anatomical equipment to produce song.)

Moreover, aesthetic ratings of the songs by human beings correlate with the physical development of the birds. We rate the Mimidae—mockingbirds, catbirds, thrashers—highly as singers, and all of them have seven pairs of vocal cord muscles, whereas most other birds have a single pair.

Though the characteristics of song are influenced by the construction of the syrinx, or vocal cord, perfected song is probably learned. Thus, the evolution of song marches right along with the evolution of the birds, from lowest to highest in development. Gulls and birds of prey, low on the evolutionary scale of birds, have almost no song, but perching birds such as thrushes, in the highest order of birds, sing a lot. Small size also tends to produce song, perhaps because songs make the singer recognizable from a distance.

Song itself is characterized by pitch, intensity, volume, and quality. Various songs are distinct by reason of timing, repetitiveness, notes, trills, and phrases. Edward A. Armstrong, a respected authority on bird song, display, and behavior, believes that two or more phrases in a regular succession may correspond to a sentence. He believes that songs communicate the location of food, water, nest sites, roosts, and predators. Moreover, they may convey information such as species, sex, individual identity, status, sexual motivation, need, aggressiveness, alarm or fear, and the location of an individual. It seems safe to assume, at least, that song gives clues to the size of the territory, the number of males in an area (since males sing more in dense population areas), and the phase of the breeding cycle.

Variations in bird song seem endless. The "whisper song" may be heard during bad weather, including periods of extreme heat, but some birds sing quietly on the nest regardless of weather. Swainson's thrushes sing the whisper song during migration, and vireos when first arriving in their territories. Blue jays sometimes sing it when they think no one is around—it wouldn't do to ruin their image as screamers.

Bird song is more common at dawn and dusk than at any other time, but you'll hear less of it during cold snaps and in periods of wind or heavy rain. Some diurnal birds—mockingbirds, nightingales, and the marsh wren—sing at night. Birds start singing when they're young; they have their full repertory of songs by the time they raise their first brood.

When defending their territory, birds sing most often from an open perch, usually at a distance from the nest, although some males sing while actually on the nest. Singing also occurs in flight. The loudness and frequency of territorial songs decline as the nesting season progresses. Although females sing less frequently than males, duets of pairs may reinforce pair bonding. Since songs are most common among birds living in dense habitat, song may help them communicate when visual contact is difficult.

Getting Down to Cases

Although transliteration of bird notes into letter combinations is occasionally incomprehensible to me, it is nevertheless a widespread practice and forms the basis of bird-song description. Accordingly—and since I have nothing better to offer—I have used it in this section in the hope it will be helpful and entertaining.

American kestrels have an excited *klee-call* when disturbed, a *whine-call* when transferring food, and a *chitter-call* during approaches and copulation. Ground doves utter their *cooo-oo* call from seven to twenty times, and the males' mating call is *koul, koul*. As the male mourning dove spreads his tail so that the white shows, he calls, closes his tail, waits, and repeats the entire procedure. His love song is transliterated as *coo-ah, coo, coo, coo, ooo; ah-coo'-roo-ooo*. The *whee-whee-whee* sound when he flies may be a song rather than a wing sound. Inca doves *coo* while head bobbing; the male song is *cut-cut-ca-doah*. The imported spotted dove has a harsh and vigorous song: *wook'-ko-whooo'*.

Male Anna's hummingbirds squeak and warble, in pursuit calling shrill chittering notes, *ztikl-ztikl-ztikl*. Both males and females make a noise that sounds like *chip*. Allen's hummingbird buzzes, hums, and squeaks.

The northern flicker calls *yuk-yuk-yuk*; the red-bellied woodpecker says *cha cha cha* or *churr, churr, churr,* and drums. Although the hairy woodpecker usually says only *peenk,* he changes his call during courtship and the defending of territory to *kuweek, kuweek, kuweek* or *tew-tew.* He also drums. The downy woodpecker's call is *pink* or a rattle; during courtship it is a low, harsh chattering cry and drumming.

Once we reach Passeriformes, the song situation becomes more complicated. Crows, which can mimic laughter and some words, have in courtship a rapid succession of sharp notes that is said to sound like the grinding of teeth. Everyone recognizes their *caw-caw-caw,* but they also say *orr-orr, ah-ah, gnaw-gnaw, kaa-wha-wha-kaa-wha-wha, nevah-nevah, ha-ha-ha,* and *chick.* Youngsters say *car-car-car.*

The repertoire of the blue jay consists of *jay-jay, tea-cup tea-cup, tull-ul, kuk-kuk-kuk,* and (surprise) includes a low, sweet song like a robin's. The gray jay also has a low, pleasant song during courtship but otherwise contents itself with eight or ten whistles, *cla-cla-cla-cla-cla-cla-cla,* and *chuck-chuck.* It is suspected that gray jays engage in mimicry. The noises (maybe technically songs!) of Steller's jay include *shaak-shaak-shaak, klooh-klooh-klooh,* and *ca-phee-ca-phee.* Clark's nutcracker makes a catlike sound written as *meack-mearck* and also says *chaar-char-r-r-churr-churr* and *kr-a-a-kar-r-r-aah.* Mates sing duets, the sound of which has been compared to toy tin trumpets; they are also mimics. Scrub jays have a large repertoire, all of it ghastly: *CA, quay-quay-quay-quay-quay-quay-quay, kwesh-kwese-kwesh-kwese-kwesh-kwese-kwesh-kwese-kwesh-kwese-kwesh-kwese-kwesh-kwese, boy'-ee-boy'-ee, tscheck-tscheck,* and *ker-wheek.* In Florida, they add *churr;* in the Rocky Mountains it's *we'-ahk.*

Still farther up the evolutionary ladder, the tufted titmouse says *peter-peter-peter, peto-peto-peto,* and *ya-ya-ya.* Black-capped chickadees say *fee-bee* (with Carolina chickadees it becomes *fee-bee-fee-bay*) and *chick-a-dee-dee-dee-dee.* (They may add up to ten *dee*'s to the *chick-a,* but four is usual.) They also make a high-pitched lisping sound written as *seep* or *stheep,* a *si-si-sisi* call, *sizzle-ee* (or *sizzle-oo*), and what has fancifully been described as a "long jingling like distant sleighbells." Mountain chickadees are said to have a hoarser quality than black-capped chickadees; their call sounds like *chick-a-chay-chay-chay* or *chick-a-zee-zee-zee.* The call of the boreal chickadee is described as more lisping, wheezy, and husky—and also louder—than the black-capped. It is written *chick-a-deer-deer, chee-chee-zay-zay, che-chit,* and *chip-chee-chee.* There is intense disagreement about its song.

The song of the red-breasted nuthatch is similar to that of the white-breasted, but higher: *ink-ink-ink, hit-hit.* The call of the brown creeper is a thin, high *seeee;* its song is *see-to-ti-see-ti-seetse-seetsay.*

With Bewick's wren we begin to encounter the real singers. Its song is beautiful, beginning high and rapid and changing to a lower register followed by trills. Its call is a high *chick-chick, kut-kut-kut*, or a harsh *spee*. The calls of the Carolina wren are described as clacks, rattles, and trills, its alarm note *CHEER-p*. Its song is loud and similar to the cardinal's (some call it the "mocking wren," although others give that title to Bewick's wren). Descriptions of the song tend toward the fanciful: *TEA-kettle-TEA-kettle-TEA-kettle*, *TWEE-dle-TWEE-dle-TWEE-dle*, and *SWEETheart-SWEETheart*.

The songs of the brown thrasher, somewhat subdued during courtship, suggest those of the mockingbird, but don't contain as much mimicry. Most phrases are repeated twice. Its call is *smaack*, and a ventriloquial *chuuuurl* when feeding its young. The song of the California thrasher is also beautiful, with much variation and some mimicry. Their relatives, the ventriloquist catbirds, have a mewing call and several notes—*chuck, chatter*, and *kak-kak-kak*—in addition to their softer, pleasing songs. The songs of the mockingbird can only be described as extraordinary. Each phrase is repeated three to six times and individual variations are common.

Thrushes have a well-deserved reputation as songsters; robins are the earliest singers of the day. Their alarm note is *tuk-tuk-tuk*. The wood thrush, which likes a high perch early in the season and a lower one later on, is an excellent singer. The hermit thrush has 150 different songs and is sometimes ventriloquial. Starlings, apparently fond of unmusical noises, nevertheless have the ability to sing beautifully. House sparrows are chirpers (*chirp, cer-eep*) rather than singers; in courtship they utter a soft, clear warble. Youngsters have a subsong and can be taught to sing, so it is assumed that the chirping is an evolutionary advance, not a failing.

Some observers describe the song of the red-winged blackbird as reedy, a thin, high whine followed by *chuck*; others cite the more familiar *kong-la-reeee* or *o-ka-leee*. The orchard oriole has an attractive song similar to that of a bobolink or fox sparrow; the northern (Baltimore) oriole gives six or seven loud whistles in announcing his territory and a loud, harsh chatter as an alarm call. The courtship song of the common grackle is a squeaky, shrill wheeze.

More pleasing, the yellow-rumped warbler has a "simple liquid rattle," whereas the rufous-sided towhee sings a noisy *Drink-your-TEA-E-E-E*. The western tanager sounds a lot like a robin. The white-throated sparrow has a beautiful song consisting of whistles, opening usually with a couple of clear notes, followed by three quavering notes of different pitch. Some people insist the bird is saying *Old Sam Peabody, Peabody, Peabody*, but then people say remarkable things sometimes. The tree sparrow says *whee-hee-ho-hee* and calls *tseet*.

The song sparrow puts all his relatives to shame, however, with his astonishing music.

He is cheerful and persistent, with great variation. The call is *chiff* or *chimp*. At least two dozen songs comprise his repertoire, all of them beginning with three to six emphasized notes. A common beginning is the first four notes of Beethoven's Fifth Symphony. Although each song sparrow has songs peculiar to itself, all use bits and pieces of their neighbors' songs. They sing to each other, and the songs sound like familiar human songs that they never get around to finishing.

Cardinals utter loud clear whistles and beautiful songs with many variations; they are sometimes confused with the songs of the Carolina wren. The song of the purple finch is rapid and jumbled, similar to that of the house finch and Cassin's finch in its cheerful and spritely warbling. Painted and indigo buntings also have finch-like songs. The American goldfinch has a loud, canary-like song; so does the pine siskin, though it's a trifle less musical.

Both male and female rose-breasted grosbeaks sing, occasionally even (softly) while on the nest. Their songs, long, smooth and liquid, have been compared favorably to that of the robin. The evening grosbeak utters short loud warbles and whistles during courtship, and the dickcissel (of course) says *dick-dick-cissel-cissel-cissel.*

A lot of this free-floating melody is leading up to something. Having proclaimed a territory and attracted a mate, the male is about to become a parent. Whether he's helpful in the next phase—nest building—depends on his species.

5 | NESTING

BIRDS ARE DESCENDANTS of reptiles and began emerging in the orders we know today during the Paleocene and Eocene eras, the earliest part of the Age of Mammals. Nest building probably developed as birds became warm-blooded and could no longer leave their eggs to hatch in the heat of the environment. Ideally, nests should protect not only the eggs but also the incubating parent. Nests are ordinarily as inconspicuous as possible, a factor in survival. Considering that the typical figure for nesting success (youngsters that achieve maturity) is 20 percent, it's obvious that nesting birds face horrendous problems.

Think of nests as cradles for eggs, nurseries for young birds. The kind of nest that a bird builds is directly related to the degree of evolution a species has achieved; it is assumed that birds and nests evolved together. The first nests, at the beginnings of bird history, were probably depressions in the ground or natural cavities in rocks, tree roots, and hollow trees. Even today some birds merely choose a *place* but don't modify it in any way—the female lays the eggs and, evidently, hopes for the best. The whip-poor-wills are one example: the female merely places her two eggs on a bed of oak leaves on the ground. The killdeer lays her eggs on a bed of wood chips, grass, gravel, or cinders and on the graveled roofs of buildings, a location also chosen by common nighthawks and one that seems a great deal more secure than the ground. Most nests, however, protect the eggs and maybe even the hatchlings.

When some birds began to elevate their nests, it became necessary for them to gather nesting materials, probably twigs and sticks, to serve as a platform. Phoebes and robins use platforms to this day. Eventually, certain birds, especially the highly developed passerines, built complicated cup-shaped nests.

Just as the world still has relatively primitive birds such as loons in addition to the entire range of more and more highly developed birds, so, too, bird nest development extends from bare gravel to the marvelous hanging nests of Africa's weaverbirds.

The best time to find and identify nests is in the winter. You'll not be disturbing any birds, and the nests are easier to find when leaves are gone from the trees and ground vegetation is not growing. You don't have to mount an expedition to look for nests, either. I'm always surprised at the number of nests I can see from my car window. Many birds build near the road, even when it's a busy interstate highway, and many nest in city parks. Wherever you see a stand, however small, of mature trees, you'll find nests. If the trees are tall enough, you'll see enormous nests. Nests of birds that prefer brambly sites are harder to spot, even after the leaves have disappeared.

Hiking and horseback riding are good ways to see nests in all their diversity. Some nests are easier to recognize than others—it's difficult to identify the bare scraping of ground that suffices for certain species. Slightly more highly developed birds line such scrapes; others use natural mounds or floating clumps of vegetation. Ground holes as well as tree holes may be nesting sites. The cup-shaped nest is considered the classic, however, and it can be found on the ground or floating on a raft or wedged in the fork of a tree. It may be domed or otherwise enclosed, suspended, or bound with mud.

Some birds, like ducks, nest communally (in the same area with other species), some are colonial, and some accept nesting boxes. Martins are colonial nesters, and are entirely willing to use birdhouses. The aforementioned weaverbird of South Africa builds apartment complexes of up to one hundred units, which belong to the flock. Ani cuckoos in tropical portions of the Americas build their basin-shaped nests as a communal home; several females lay eggs in the nest and the whole community cares for the young, which in turn may stay and help out with the next brood. Except for seabirds, birds usually nest in their feeding territory. The site of the nest is a major clue in the identification of its owner.

Choosing the site of the nest and building it are dominated by the female. In polygamous species, the female does it all, but monogamous birds often share equally or divide the tasks. Each species makes a distinctive type of nest, and there is considerable variation in the materials used. On the whole, birds use readily available materials, which itself accounts for variation depending on location. Some birds nest, for protection, close to an aggressive species of animal. A few of the cavity-nesters also use their nest sites as roosts and shelters.

The type of nest used by a species is thought to be intrinsic, but some learning of techniques apparently takes place because first-time builders are less skillful than the experienced. Those birds that build new quarters for additional broods spend less time and energy on each successive nest. Nests may take a day or weeks to build, depending on the length of the breeding season. Some birds continue adding to their nests after they are in use. The time spent on building a nest also varies with weather and area; for example, birds in the Arctic spend less time on the chore than birds in temperate climates do.

Birds that collect food in their claws also collect and transport their building materials in that way; those that use their bills to collect food use them to collect nesting material as well. Nesting materials are usually some kind of plant, but mud, animal hair, and feathers are also used. Hummingbirds and parula warblers use spider silk to strengthen their nests. Some birds incorporate cellophane, tissues, yarn, and newspapers into their nests. Hawks decorate them with green leaves, replaced regularly. Linings, if any, are often soft and warm.

Sometimes nesting materials can harm the nestlings. Birders are warned not to offer nesting materials such as long pieces of string or yarn that might strangle a bird. We had a catastrophe in our barn last summer. A barn swallow pair had used horsehair in their nest, and one morning we found a dead fledgling whose feet had become entangled in it hanging from the nest.

In North America, northern (Baltimore) orioles, bushtits, and woodpeckers build the most complicated nests. In other parts of the world, however, there are even more complex bird nests. Birds are highly adaptable and build deeper nests in places subject to strong winds, for example. Some bird nests are so tiny that the incubating bird hides them; some are so enormous that the bird disappears within them. The records for large nests in North America go to a bald eagle family in Vermillion, Ohio, whose nest was 12 feet deep, 8-1/2 feet in diameter, and weighed two tons, and a pair in Florida that used a nest 20 feet deep and 9-1/2 feet across.

Most passerines build a new nest for each brood, but wrens, hawks, eagles, and owls will use the same nest for years, and bluebirds will use the same nestbox over and over. Certain tree cavity-nesters don't excavate their nest sites but use whatever cavity is available. Some use abandoned woodpecker nest holes; hawks and great horned owls will appropriate an abandoned eagle, hawk, or osprey nest. Occasionally birds use old nests for winter shelter. Robins may use an old nest as a foundation for a new one. Occasionally up to three chimney swifts or three cliff swallows will use the same nest—some birders speculate that a sort of apprenticeship is involved.

Getting Down to Cases

Here's a rundown on the nests of specific birds—where you're likely to find them, and what they're made from. We'll begin with the most primitive birds, the loons, most like their remote ancestors, and work up to the most advanced, the passerines, or perching birds.

Loon nests are most likely to be found on small wooded islands in freshwater lakes throughout the northern United States, Canada, and Alaska. They consist of a loose collection of rushes, grass, twigs, and reeds and may be on bare ground, a floating bog, a muskrat house, or in shoreline vegetation. The Canada goose nest is merely a depression lined with sticks, grass, reeds, and down. The female builds it on the ground near water.

Mallard nests are also usually on the ground near water, in woods or brush. Sometimes they are found in tall grass or in alfalfa fields. The inside diameter of the depression on dry ground is 8 inches, and the nest is made of grass, leaves, and reeds. The female selects the site and builds alone, starting to lay on bare ground and gradually assembling more and more nesting materials, constructing her nest as she incubates and placing down over the eggs when she leaves them. The wood duck, which accepts nesting boxes, nests in a tree

Birds in the saguaro country of the southwestern United States excavate holes in the cactus for nests. After a time, the plant forms scar tissue over the wound. The Apaches once used this bulbous scar tissue for water jugs; now they use it as birdboxes.

cavity from 3 to 60 feet up, in wooded swamps or marshes or beside water. The cavity is lined with wood chips and down.

Black vultures don't bother with a nest at all; the eggs are laid in hollow stumps, thickets, and caves. Turkey vultures lay theirs on the ground, in gravel, or in sawdust. A bald eagle pair builds its eyrie together, in the fork of a giant tree. It's a huge pile of sticks and branches lined with grass, moss, sod, and weeds. They may use the same one for years, and continue adding to it until eventually it topples of its own weight. It starts out being 2 feet high and about 5 feet in diameter.

The female northern harrier builds on or near the ground in freshwater or saltwater marshes or other wet places. The male gathers the material—sticks, straw, and dry grasses— for the 2- to 18-inch-high structure. Ospreys nest in loose colonies near fresh or salt water. The nests may be near the ground or up to 60 feet high, on trees or poles. Often used for years, they're constructed of small to enormous sticks and lined with bark, sod, and grass. Kestrels, which accept nesting boxes, are cavity-nesters, using tree holes 15 to 30 feet from the ground with a hole 2 to 4 inches in diameter. They do not line the cavity. Flickers and squirrels compete with them for nesting holes.

The nest of the northern bobwhite is built by both parents in a hollow in the grass and is lined with grasses. They weave weeds into an arch over the nest. Ruffed grouse nest under logs or at the base of a tree in hollows they line with leaves or pine needles. Ring-necked pheasants nest on the ground in a natural hollow lined with weeds, grasses, and leaves. Turkeys nest in a depression in dead leaves on dry ground. The spotted sandpiper lays her eggs, usually near water, on the ground in a saucer-like depression.

American woodcock, found in damp woods, nest 300 feet from the singing ground (the area above which the male performs his courtship flight song) in an unconcealed depression in dead leaves rimmed with twigs and lined with pine needles. The colonial herring gull nests in open, sandy areas on the ground. Both parents scrape a shallow depression and then build a nest of grasses, seaweed, shells, and feathers, with an inside diameter of 8 to 10 inches.

Doves and pigeons are not impressive nest builders or nest keepers. Rock doves nest in colonies or singly, on ledges, bridges, or barns. The nest is a shallow, flimsy platform carelessly constructed of short twigs, grasses, straw, and debris of various sorts. The outside diameter is 8 inches. Female mourning doves build a frail platform of twigs, which the male collects, on a horizontal branch 3 to 20 feet above the ground. It may be lined with small twigs, pine needles, and grasses. Sometimes the female simply lays her eggs on the ground instead of in a nest; sometimes she uses an old robin, grackle, or blue jay nest. Whatever the nest, mourning doves don't clean it, and it quickly becomes a mess.

Ground doves are even dirtier, especially when they use old mourning dove nests. Sometimes they build a loose foundation of twigs or pine needles lined with rootlets and grasses placed in a vine or bush or on a stump, fence post, or horizontal branch. Other times, they nest on the ground in a slight depression, which is lined with grasses in a haphazard manner, if at all. Whatever they use, on the ground or up to 25 feet above it, the same nest serves for all the broods of a given season.

The spotted dove builds a shallow platform of sticks across the horizontal fork of a tree, usually a deciduous one. Inca doves spend about three days building a loose, shallow, cup-shaped nest of twigs, grasses, rootlets, and plant fibers. The male collects the nesting materials and passes them to the female, who puts them in place. The nest is unlined, and may be from 5 to 25 feet from the ground, in a bush, vine, or tree, on a horizontal fork. The female shapes the interior of the nest with her body.

Barn-owls don't build nests; the female lays her eggs on owl castings (disgorged encapsulated fecal material) in cavities, usually in barns, silos, or steeples. Screech owls are less consistent. Cavity-nesters, too, they lay eggs on leaves, rubble, or whatever happens to be in the cavity; they accept nestboxes in trees, especially in orchards.

Chimney swifts are partial to dark areas, especially chimneys. The nest, a frail, thin half-saucer 4 inches in diameter and attached to the inside of a structure, is built of twigs gathered in flight, broken off trees, by both parents. The twigs are held together by a glutinous secretion from the bird's mouth, popularly called "saliva," though it isn't, of course. It hardens and binds the twigs together and attaches the nest to the wall. Chimney swifts will use old nests, repaired. The female puts the finishing touches to the nest while incubating.

Vaux's swift, which formerly nested only near the bottom of a hollow tree, is now also using chimneys. The white-throated swift nests on dry cliffs; the black swift uses a site on

Owl with family in eagles' nest.

a mountainside. They are so successful in choosing places difficult to reach that the first recorded nest was not found until 1901.

Hummingbirds, which build beautiful nests, also use a saliva-like glue to attach their nests to the chosen site. The nest of the ruby-throated hummingbird is an inch deep and an inch in diameter (about the size of an eyecup) and is built from 5 to 50 feet high, on a small limb of a tree in orchard or woods, often over water. The nest is made of bud scales covered with lichens and is lined with plant down, the whole held together by spider or caterpillar silk. Old nests are renewed the following season. Other hummingbirds build similar nests.

Allen's hummingbird usually chooses a height of 12 feet for its nest, but the nests have been found anywhere from 1 to 90 feet from the ground. The Lucifer hummingbird chooses a site in a shrub, up to 6 feet from the ground, for a nest of plant down bound with cobwebs and decorated with lichens. Costa's hummingbird uses shreds of dried leaves, bark, lichens, and plant down for a nest bound by spiderweb and decorated with lichens, placed in a shrub from 1 to 9 feet from the ground. The blue-throated hummingbird attaches its nest of plant down and moss bound by spiderweb to a flower stalk or other slender stalk on a stream bank.

The violet-crowned hummingbird hangs a nest of cottony plant fibers decorated with lichens on a hanging sycamore twig. Anna's hummingbird uses lichens or mosses—lined with feathers or fur—in its nest, which is often placed on a branch near or over water, 2 to 30 feet from the ground. The female continues building it as she incubates the eggs. The black-chinned hummingbird likes a site near water, too, from 4 to 30 feet from the ground in a willow, sycamore, or (in arid country) cottonwood tree. The nest, made of plant down usually without lichen decoration, resembles a tiny yellow sponge. Rufous hummingbirds sometimes nest close together, 2 to 20 feet from the ground. Sometimes they build a new nest on top of an old one.

Belted kingfishers nest in a burrow in a bank, near water. Excavation takes them two to three weeks. An interesting feature of the burrow is its 3-1/2- to 4-inch-diameter tunnel entrance. The burrow itself may be 6 or 7 feet long.

Northern flickers, also cavity-nesters, readily accept birdhouses mounted on poles facing south. Normally they nest 2 to 90 feet from the ground in a cavity 7 to 8 inches in diameter with a 3-inch entrance hole. To attract them to a nestbox, put wood chips, their choice of material in natural conditions, on the bottom of the box.

Red-bellied woodpeckers build a gourd-shaped nest 12 to 18 inches deep in a dead tree, anywhere from 50 to 130 feet from the ground. It takes them a week to ten days to excavate the interior to their design. The entrance hole is 1-3/4 to 2 inches in diameter. Downy woodpeckers make a similar nest, 8 to 12 inches deep, with a 1-1/4-inch entrance hole. They nest 5 to 30 feet from the ground.

Ornithologists think the female hairy woodpecker selects the site for a nest, usually new for each season, but both parents excavate. It takes them one to three weeks to fashion the gourd-shaped nest, which is 5 to 60 feet from the ground and a foot deep, with an entrance hole 1-7/8 by 1-1/2 inches. The female lays her eggs in wood chips.

Eastern kingbirds build their rough, bulky nests on a tree limb away from the trunk, using weeds and grasses lined with fine grasses. The dimensions are 5-1/2 inches in diameter and 3-1/4 inches high. Eastern phoebes prefer shelf-like projections on bridges or buildings as nest sites. The female builds a circular or semicircular nest in anywhere from three to thirteen days. It is large—4-1/2 inches in diameter and 4 inches high—and well made of weeds, grasses, and mud covered with moss and lined with fine grasses and hair.

Swallows may use nests from previous years—they're deep cups lined with grasses and feathers. Barn swallows often nest in colonies around or in buildings, bridges, and culverts. (Formerly they used caves in cliffs.) They plaster the mud-and-straw structures to beams and use feathers, preferably white, for the lining. The top of the nest is semicircular, 5 inches in diameter, and it tapers downward in a cone shape. It takes them six to eight days to build a new one, less time to repair an old one.

Tree swallows use a tree hole or nestbox 5 to 10 feet from the ground with a 1-1/2-inch entrance hole. It takes the female up to two weeks (some sources say up to a month) to build the nest of dry grasses lined with feathers; the male gathers some of the material. Tree swallows may be solitary nesters or they may nest in groups. Purple martins nest in dense colonies, 15 to 20 feet from the ground. Both parents build the nest, using grasses, twigs, bark, paper, leaves, and string.

That brings us to the Corvidae. Common ravens are solitary nesters who build their large structures in coniferous trees, on cliffs or rock ledges, often on top of last year's nest. Their deeply hollowed nests are built of branches, sticks, twigs, and grapevines and thickly lined with hair, moss, grasses, and bark shreds. They are 6 inches deep and 2 to 4 feet in diameter.

Crows build large bulky nests, too. Cup-shaped and made of sticks, they are lined with bark, vegetable fibers, rootlets, grasses, and moss. At times they use feathers, cornstalks, string, cloth, and seaweed. They are usually 30 feet from the ground, but the height may vary from 10 to 100 feet. They particularly like pines or oaks near a clearing. The nests are 7 inches high and about 2 feet in diameter. Sometimes the crows are evicted by a great horned owl; other times a long-eared owl may use an abandoned crow's nest.

Blue jays build coarse, careless, cup-shaped nests with ragged brims hidden in a crotch or outer branch, usually 10 to 20 feet from the ground, although the height may vary from 5 to 50 feet. They prefer evergreens. Both parents build, with thorny twigs, rootlets, bark, moss, leaves, paper, rags, and string and a lining of bark, grasses, leaves, and feathers. Nests are 7 or 8 inches in diameter, 4 to 4-1/2 inches high. Both gather materials from the ground, but the males also break twigs from trees. The building takes about five days, and the female does a bigger share than the male.

Steller's jay builds a large, bulky, bowl-shaped nest of sticks, mud, and grasses lined with rootlets, pine needles, and grasses on a platform of old leaves in the crotch of a tree from 2 to 100 feet from the ground, but most often 8 to 25 feet up. Scrub jays may build in scattered colonies with up to six nests or in solitary. Together the pair form oak twigs into thick-walled cups lined with rootlets. It takes them about five days, and they prefer a lower site—4 to 12 feet high—than blue jays. In Florida, the nest is small and well built and the walls may contain stems and leaves as well as twigs; the lining may have wool, moss, and feathers in addition to rootlets. In the West, scrub jays build a bulkier nest and add horsehair to the lining.

Gray jays nest early—late February to April—and build bulky, high-walled nests of twigs, grasses, and bark lined with moss, lichens, plant down, and feathers. Nests are held together with cocoons and spiderwebs and are usually 4 to 10 feet from the ground, though they have been found as high as 30 feet up. The nests of Clark's nutcracker are found under an evergreen branch and are similar to those of the jays.

Tufted titmice are cavity-nesters who like a 1-1/2-inch entrance hole 3 to 30 feet from the ground, though they're known to nest as high as 97 feet up. Both build the cupped nest, of leaves, bark, moss, grasses, cotton, wool, string, cloth, feathers, fur, and old snakeskins. They even pluck hair from live animals for their nests. They will accept nestboxes.

Black-capped chickadees share in the excavation of a cavity (males and females carry the wood chips away from the site and drop them), but the female makes the nest itself, of moss, vegetable fibers, cinnamon fern, wood chips, feathers, cocoons, hair, fur, and wool. They like a 1-inch entrance hole, in a site 4 to 15 feet from the ground. Sometimes, for reasons unknown, they abandon the nest and start a new one somewhere else. They are especially fond of birch snags, which are easily pierced and excavated although the papery bark holds the rotten wood together. They accept nesting boxes.

Carolina chickadees like a cavity 6 to 15 feet from the ground. The nest is built on a foundation of moss, grasses, and bark and lined with vegetable down, feathers, hair, and fur. One side, higher than the others, serves as a flap which is pulled down over the eggs when a parent is off the nest. Mountain chickadees nest in evergreen forests in cavities 1 to 15 feet from the ground. The entrance hole is an inch in diameter, the cavity 9 inches deep. The nest is made of grasses, moss, plant down, bark, rootlets, squirrel and rabbit fur, cow or deer hair, and sheep's wool. Boreal chickadees nest in cavities or stumps 6 inches deep and 1 to 10 feet from the ground and make their nests of moss, lichens, bark, and fern down, lining them with feathers or fur.

The brown creeper nests under loose flakes of bark on a tree, 5 to 15 feet from the ground. The male gathers materials for the nest, and the female builds—it takes her up to a month. The shape of the nest, made of a foundation of twigs, leaves, and bark lined with grasses and moss, conforms to the space. Its center is neatly cupped; the sides have points.

White-breasted nuthatches want a hole 2 to 60 feet from the ground and 6 inches deep and will accept nestboxes. The female builds the nest of loose bark with grasses, twigs, rootlets, bark, and feathers on top, lined with hair sometimes plucked from a live animal. The male brings the female the materials and feeds her. Red-breasted nuthatches also accept nestboxes. They need entrance holes an inch in diameter (around which they smear pitch, for some reason). The nest is of wood chips, sometimes with feathers, grasses, rootlets, and bark added.

The original Indian name for wrens meant "big noise from little size." Noisy house wrens use cavities for nests, whether in trees, birdhouses, or elsewhere. The male cleans out the nest site (sometimes destroying the nestlings of another bird in the process) and makes a foundation of twigs. The female forms a cup of grasses, rootlets, feathers, hair—and assorted rubbish. As mentioned in the Courtship chapter, a male winter wren builds several nests and shows them to a female, who chooses the one she prefers. The female lines the nest with soft plant fibers before she lays her eggs.

Carolina wrens choose a cranny near the ground, usually less than 10 feet up, although 40 feet up has been reported. The nest is a bulky affair of twigs, grasses, and leaves lined with finer materials. It is 6 inches deep and roofed, with a side entrance, if it's built in the open. Bewick's wren uses a crevice, generally 6 feet up but anywhere from 3 to 25 feet from the ground. In a large structure composed mostly of rubbish and bark, the wren makes a compact, strong, deep cup. The project takes ten days.

Brown thrashers nest on the ground and up to 14 feet from the ground, preferably in tangled growth. On a loose foundation of thorny twigs, both parents build a large cup of dry leaves, followed by an inner cup of grasses and twigs which is then lined with rootlets. The diameter is 1 foot, and the height 3-3/4 inches. It takes them five to seven days.

Catbirds like similar brambly sites, normally not more than 10 feet from the ground (but nests have been reported 20 to 60 feet up). Their concealed nests, built by both parents in five to six or eight days, are deep, good-sized, scraggly-looking, cup-shaped structures made of twigs, vines, cedar bark, weeds, leaves, and grasses lined with rootlets. (Some authorities say that the male merely helps in gathering materials and that all the actual building is done by the female.) Its appearance is quite similar to a mockingbird's nest, but catbirds use fewer manufactured materials. They may use the same nest for second and third broods.

The nests of mockingbirds are usually 3 to 10 feet from the ground, in a bush or shrub, but nests have been reported from 1 to 30 feet from the ground. The nest is bulky, its outer shell of thorny twigs and its inner construction of leaves, weeds, bark, rootlets, string, rags, cotton, paper, mosses, and hair lined with fine grasses, plant down, horsehair, and rootlets. Both parents build the nest, which is 7 inches in diameter and 4-1/2 inches high, in one to four days. Generally, the male gathers more of the material and the female does more building.

Robins nest nearly anywhere, often in a place very inconvenient for their human neighbors. The nest is cup-shaped, made of twigs cemented with mud and lined with fine grasses or, preferably, domestic animal fur. It is usually 5 to 30 feet from the ground, often in evergreens because robins nest early, when the leaves of the deciduous trees have not yet appeared. It takes two to six days (a high of twenty days has been reported) to build the nest, which has an inside diameter of 4 inches. Male robins alternate between helping the female build the nest and singing to defend the territory. The female smooths the lining with her breast.

The wood thrush builds a nest much like that of the robin. It, too, is a large cup made of grasses, leaves, weeds, and moss held together with rotted leaves or mud and lined with fine grasses or rootlets. It is most likely to be found in the fork of a tree 3 to 12 feet from the ground, though nests have been reported as high as 50 feet up. Interestingly, the wood thrush often puts something white on the nest's outer wall.

The hermit thrush builds near the ground in damp, cool woods. The compact, cup-shaped nest may be from 3 to 10 feet from the ground. It has a bulky exterior made of twigs, grasses, bark, weeds, ferns, and moss lined with pine needles, rootlets, or porcupine hair.

Tufted titmouse will accept nesting boxes.

Eastern bluebirds, cavity-nesters, make loose nests of fine grass. The female builds the nest in four or five days. Its outside diameter varies; it is usually about 2 inches high.

Cedar waxwings build on a horizontal limb 4 to 50 feet from the ground. Their loose nest is composed of grasses, twigs, string, and yarn lined with rootlets and fine grasses. Both parents build, taking five to seven days. The nest is 4-1/2 to 6 inches in diameter, 3-1/2 to 4-1/2 inches high. Shrikes nest in thorny, brambly places.

Starlings nest on buildings or in trees 10 to 30 feet from the ground; nests have been reported from 2 to 60 feet up, however. They're cavity-nesters. The male appears on the site first, clears out anything that might be in the cavity, and brings dead leaves, bark, moss, lichens, green leaves, and tree flowers to the chosen place. The female comes along and throws out all he's brought and in a few days builds a nest to her satisfaction, mostly of grasses, although weeds, leaves, and cloth may be added. The lining is of fine grasses and feathers. Some observers report that it is built in a slovenly manner and is carelessly kept. (A bad reputation taints everything.) In any case, she builds a new one for each brood. Nests may be solitary or in colonies.

Female red-eyed vireos build nests noted for their beauty. In four or five days, they select the site, gather materials, and build a nest with a 2-inch inside diameter of bark, grasses, and spider egg cases lined with plant down. Yellow-rumped warblers build from 5 to 30 feet from the ground in a spruce or fir tree. The male brings a little material for building, but the construction falls to the female, who uses dried grasses, weeds, and bark bound by spiderwebs and lined with hair or plant down. It takes her about a week.

The common yellowthroat nests in the brush of open fields, on the ground or to a height of about 2 feet. Made of grasses and leaves and lined with grasses and hair, the inside diameter of the nest measures 1-1/4 inches. One source says that the only warbler likely to nest in a garden is the yellow warbler. They especially like willows and alders, wild roses and grapes for their site, preferably about 10 feet from the ground.

The house sparrow will nest in a cavity in a tree, a crevice in a building, or elsewhere, usually from 10 to 30 feet from the ground. The nest resembles a huge ball of grasses, weeds, and assorted trash, and has an opening on the side. It's large, bulky, and loosely constructed. Both parents build (some observers insist that the female alone builds), lining the nest with feathers, hair, or string. This lined part is at the center and is relatively compact. Nests vary in size, depending on the area of the site. Sometimes, like wrens and blackbirds, they take over the nest of another species, destroying the eggs or young. House sparrows are very sociable, and frequently four or five nests are found close together in a small tree. Truly monogamous and quite sedentary, these homebodies use their nests as year-round homes.

Red-winged blackbirds are social nesters, building in loose colonies containing anywhere from a few to several hundred pairs. Although they are gregarious, they vigorously defend the territory of the nest itself for a few cubic yards, striking at intruders. The female selects the actual site, which is low and near water. The cup-shaped nest is made of long strands of rushes, grasses, and moss, plastered with mud and bound to the surrounding vegetation with milkweed fibers and lined with fine grasses. She spends three to six days in gathering material and in construction. The nest usually is 3 to 8 feet from the ground, often suspended, usually in a shrub. Some nests have been observed in trees as much as 30 feet from the ground; others are on the ground.

Female northern (Baltimore) orioles select the site for their nests, usually on a tree branch hanging over a clearing. It takes five or six days for her to build a hanging, gourd-shaped nest about 5 inches long. Its outer shell is tightly woven of weed stalks and inner bark and perhaps string. The bottom is filled with plant down or hair. The female bounces in the nest, using her breast to shape it. The orchard oriole's nest does not swing free. The female builds the large rounded nest with a constructed rim, of weeds, fibers, and dried grasses.

Common grackles are somewhat colonial in nesting habits. They are partial to evergreens, 3 to 30 feet from the ground. The female builds the loose, bulky nest, which has an inside diameter of 4 inches, an outside diameter of 7 to 9 inches, and is 5 to 8 inches high. Sometimes she builds on an osprey nest. Her own is well made, of twigs, coarse grasses, and seaweed, lined and cemented with mud and lined again with soft grasses and feathers. It may take the parents up to six weeks to gather materials, but the female does the building in about five days.

Female scarlet tanagers build a small, flimsy, flat cup of a nest on a tree limb, preferably oak, out from the trunk and from 8 to 75 feet from the ground. It is made of twigs and rootlets, lined with grasses. That of summer tanagers is similar in shape but typically is made of grasses, rootlets, leaves, bark, and Spanish moss, lined with fine grasses. The female usually builds it 5 to 20 feet from the ground, although nests have been reported as much as 60 feet from the ground. It takes her about two weeks. Western tanagers build frail, 5-inch-wide, saucer-shaped nests of grasses, bark, and twigs lined with rootlets and hair. They may be placed 3 to 25 feet from the trunk of the tree and 5 to 30 feet from the ground.

The female cardinal builds a loose nest of twigs, leaves, weeds, bark, and grasses lined with hair, rootlets, and fine grasses in three to nine days. She chooses the site, usually about 8 feet from the ground but sometimes as high as 30 feet. The male brings the materials.

The loose, saucer-shaped nests of the rose-breasted grosbeaks are made of twigs, weeds, and grasses lined with finer materials and placed 5 to 20 feet from the ground. Evening grosbeaks are relatively social in their nesting and prefer conifers as sites, 15 to 60 feet from the ground. The frail, elliptical cups are made of twigs and moss, 5 to 5-7/8 inches in diameter and 5 inches high. The lining is made of grasses or rootlets.

Indigo buntings make good cup-shaped nests of dried grasses, twigs, leaves, and weeds lined with fine grasses, hair, feathers, and rootlets on a base of leaves or snakeskin. They're 3-1/4 to 4-1/2 inches in diameter and 2-1/2 to 3 inches high. They are usually hidden in underbrush or a thicket, 4 to 12 feet from the ground. The birds may use the same nest for as long as five years, repairing it as needed. Painted buntings choose a site in thick foliage, usually

3 to 6 feet but sometimes as high as 20 feet from the ground. The cup-shaped nest is constructed of twigs, leaves, rootlets, bark, weeds, and grasses bound with caterpillar silk and lined with fine grasses, rootlets, and horsehair. It is similar to an indigo bunting's nest, but neater.

Dickcissel nests are built by the female about 15 feet from the ground. The nests are large and bulky, made of weeds and grasses lined with softer materials. The American goldfinch chooses leafy bushes or trees, preferably with four upright branches or a fork, 1 to 33 feet from the ground, for their tightly woven nests of milkweed with rims of bark, the whole thing bound with spider silk. Sometimes they use materials from other nests. The female spends four to five days building the cup-shaped nest 2-7/8 inches in diameter and 2-3/4 inches high.

Purple finches nest 5 to 60 feet from the ground on a horizontal branch of a conifer. The female gathers most of the material, though the male brings a bit, too. The female does all the building of the neat cup made of twigs, weeds, grasses, and bark and lined with fine grasses or hair. House finches will nest just about anywhere, including on large buildings. Materials are twigs, grasses, and debris of various kinds.

Pine siskins build a shallow saucer concealed in an evergreen 8 to 30 feet from the ground. It is made of twigs, bark, and moss densely lined with fur, hair, plant down, and moss.

Female rufous-sided towhees usually build, on or near the ground, bulky but firm nests of leaves, weeds, twigs, ferns, moss, rootlets, bark, and grasses lined with fine grasses, pine needles, and hair. Building takes about five days. The dark-eyed (slate-colored) junco makes a bulky nest on the ground under weeds and grasses, on a slope. The female constructs it of grasses, rootlets, moss, and bark shreds lined with grasses and cow or deer hair. The dark-eyed (Oregon) junco builds a similar nest but prefers a hollow in the ground to a slope.

Chipping sparrows nest in trees, vines, or shrubbery, usually 1 to 25 (but up to 40) feet from the ground. The nest is made of fine grasses, weeds, twigs, and rootlets, lined with fine grasses and cow, horse, or deer hair. Both parents build, in three or four days. The nest is 4-3/8 inches in diameter and 2-1/4 inches high. The field sparrow nests from ground level to a height of 10 feet and makes its nest of grasses, weeds, and rootlets lined with grasses and hair in three to five days. Fox sparrows build on the ground and up to 12 feet; their cup-shaped nests are made of grasses, moss, weeds, bark, and rootlets and lined with feathers, grasses, and rootlets.

Song sparrows nest on or near the ground, in shrubs or high weeds. The female builds the cup-shaped nest of grasses, bark, and leaves gathered by both parents. The inside diameter of the cup, which takes about two days to build, is 2-1/4 inches; the outside diameter is a relatively enormous 5 to 9 inches, and it's 4-1/2 inches high. It is lined with grasses, hair, and rootlets. White-crowned sparrows nest on the ground. The nests are made of small twigs, grasses, leaves, rootlets, and moss and lined with fur, hair, fine grasses, bark, and rootlets. Female white-throated sparrows build cups of grasses, twigs, leaves, and moss lined with grasses, rootlets, and hair. Tree sparrows nest in thickets and make bulky cups of grasses, rootlets, weeds, bark, and feathers lined with animal hair or fur.

Creating Yard Appeal

Two inches of 4" stovepipe around pole of birdhouse solves raccoon problem.

Attracting nesting birds to your property is no great chore, but making sure that certain features are included in the environment greatly increases your chance of success. The best single way of enticing a variety of nesting birds is to include shrubby hedgerows in the landscape design. In addition to providing shelter, they can offer various kinds of natural food. Common honeysuckle and Hansen's bush cherries are prime examples, as are currants, gooseberries, and wild or cultivated blueberries, if you're willing to share them. A patch of weeds is wonderfully appealing to birds, regardless of how homeowners feel about its aesthetic value. In fact, a bit of untidiness in the landscape increases its appeal to wild birds. Brush heaps and briar patches are also of value to them.

You can actively help nesting birds by planting trees and bushes that provide nesting sites, shelter, and food. Doubtless you're willing to let the birds enjoy the seeds of conifers. Towhees, goldfinches, and tanagers eat pine seeds, as do the aptly named crossbills. Finches like the seeds of spruces; songbirds and game birds both enjoy eating beechnuts, as well as the seeds of balsam firs. Hardwoods produce bird food, too—acorns from the oaks for jays and thrashers, woodpeckers and nuthatches; the winged seeds of maples for grosbeaks, finches, siskins; and seeds of the sweet gum for many songbirds. Hummingbirds will visit the blossoms of flowering quince for nectar. Birds such as woodpeckers and creepers will be attracted to insects on your trees.

Bird visits to your kitchen garden may count as depredations, but clover and dandelions in your yard may attract game birds. The lawn itself is useful to common grackles and starlings hunting insects and robins looking for earthworms. Aside from that, an open expanse protects the birds at your feeders or birdbaths because it doesn't afford cover for predators. Different levels of vegetation add to the allure, and so does the actual planting of foods just for the birds.

If you decide to plant bird-food crops, it's preferable to place them in several long rows, producing more edge—you will recall that the edge effect is important in attracting birds of various kinds. Millet and sunflowers are two favorite bird foods you can grow easily.

If you add a "dusting" area—a 3-by-3-foot open space with "dust" made of equal parts of sand, loam, and sifted ash to a depth of 6 inches—your real estate will appreciate considerably from the point of view of game birds such as pheasants and grouse, which like to bathe in dust just as much as chickens do. Of the common garden birds, however, only house sparrows like dust baths.

Pruning can create crotches in bushes and trees to provide support for the nests of sparrows, finches, and warblers. Sometimes artificial aids are better than natural conditions because they help to exclude the bird's natural enemies. Creating tree cavities by drilling 2-inch-deep holes into the heartwood, especially in rotten trees, will attract chickadees. Try to choose a place about 3 inches below a stout branch. Another technique is cutting a 3-inch-diameter branch 6 inches from the tree trunk. The branch will rot, forming a natural cavity.

Some of the plants in your garden may supply nesting material for birds. I don't recommend thistles or milkweed for the down that American goldfinches use in their nests, but some herbs—yarrow, rue, thyme, and pyrethrum especially—appeal to birds. Interestingly, these herbs have insecticidal properties.

Some birds can be induced to nest on your property if you provide nesting boxes or platforms for them. About fifty species accept birdhouses; of that number, thirty-five regularly do so. Specifications for birdhouses, predator guards, shelves, martin houses, martin house anchors, and an all-purpose table are given in the chapter "Learning to be a Landlord" in my book *Feeding the Birds* (Storey Communications, Inc., 1983).

Nineteenth-century England pioneered the regular use of martin houses. They seem to appeal mightily to many because of their impressive appearance and the supposed value of martins in keeping down mosquito populations. It might be well to remind potential hosts that martins and mosquitoes are not necessarily active at the same time, so the effect of one upon the other is probably minimal, despite the claims of martin-house manufacturers. A bat house (there *are* such things) might be more appropriate.

You will, of course, want to make birdhousing secure, protecting the birds from cats, raccoons, and snakes. The young of most cavity-nesters (the typical users of birdboxes) are born naked and helpless; to survive they need all the aid we can give them. Raccoons are the most common nest predators. Two inches of 4-inch stovepipe around the pole on which a birdhouse rests (or greasing the pole) will solve the problem and deter cats and snakes, too. A 3-inch collar of galvanized metal around a tree trunk is useful for the same purpose.

Housekeeping is necessary in birdhouses; removal of the contents of the house at the end of the nesting season will cut down on parasites such as mites and lice and will discourage mice from nesting there. Clean between broods, too, removing infertile eggs and dead nestlings, because otherwise the birds will make a new nest on top of the old one, and, being higher, it will be more vulnerable to predators. A mesh platform of 3/8-inch hardware cloth at the bottom of the box will let blowfly larvae drop through and prevent them from parasitizing the birds. Some birders recommend removing the nests of any "undesirables" (such as starlings and house sparrows) that invade houses; others suggest blocking the entrance holes until the species you've targeted arrives on the scene.

Features you can easily provide will attract birds and make your birdhouses desirable residences. Ventilation holes drilled near the top of the sides will provide fresh air and prevent the interior from being totally dark—a bird might spook if it flew to the entrance hole and found the insides pitch black. Wood chips or shavings on the bottom of the box will be welcome to the bird, but sawdust isn't generally recommended. For chickadees and small woodpeckers, completely fill the box with shavings and let the bird make its own cavity.

Certain considerations in placement encourage birds to use the boxes provided. Mounting the boxes on poles discourages predators, but houses for forest species, such as woodpeckers and chickadees, must be mounted directly on trees. A clear flight path to the entrance is desirable. However, the entrance hole shouldn't be exposed to windy storms, which are mostly from the east. Facing the hole to the south, southwest, or west is best. The box should be vertical or slanted slightly toward the ground to keep it from flooding.

Specific requirements vary considerably. Wood duck houses need ventilation holes in the bottom and bedding 4 inches deep, either wood shavings or sawdust. Birds in arid regions benefit from roosting sites as well as housing. Great horned owls, long-eared owls, and great gray owls will nest in chicken-wire baskets 1 or 2 inches deep supported on boards or poles. The baskets need sticks inside and should be lined with coniferous branches and a layer of twigs, leaves, and moss. The area around the nest should be fairly open for a distance of 15 to 25 feet. Screech owl boxes can be strapped to the underside of a branch; if there's no angled branch, mount the box itself at an angle. Mourning doves will use a cone-shaped nesting platform of 1/4-inch or 3/8-inch hardware cloth placed in forked branches 6 to 16 feet from the ground.

Barred owls will nest in square or round boxes 20 to 24 inches high and 12 inches square or in diameter. Drill a 6-inch hole for an entrance, put several inches of wood chips, dried leaves, or moss in the bottom, and hang it 17 feet high in a large tree.

Barn swallows, robins, and phoebes like shelves or platforms under the eaves. Make the shelf 6 inches square and 8 to 10 feet above the ground for the robins and barn swallows; for the phoebes, it should be 6 by 8 inches and 6 to 15 feet up.

Bluebird houses need an open area with about 50 feet clear to the nearest tree or perch, for the first flight of the fledglings. If you place the house away from bushes, you'll avoid possible occupancy by wrens. You can use pairs of boxes if you have tree swallows or violet-green swallows as well as bluebirds. The species will coexist in the same territory, although two pairs of the same species will not. Use a 1-1/2-inch entrance hole to exclude starlings, and place a 3/4-inch block over it so they can't reach in and peck eggs or young. It won't discourage the house sparrows, though, who need only a 1-1/8-inch entrance. If you place the nestbox far from house and barn and plug the hole until the bluebirds arrive, the house sparrows (always around) will find other quarters. The same technique is useful for martin houses. Bluebird houses shouldn't have a perching peg beneath the entrance hole, because bird marauders may use it for a site from which to harass the occupants. Houses out in the open should be light colored in order to prevent overheating.

Don't create a bird slum—four to five houses per acre is about right; even the purple martin would prefer a lower density than that commonly offered.

As a considerate host you should do your best to prevent overheating, chilling, leaking, and condensation. Use brown, tan, or gray for the exterior finish, but make sure you don't use creosote or lead-based paints. White is recommended for martin houses only because they're large, compartmented houses, sometimes made of metal and wholly out in the open. White helps to keep the temperature down. The interior of birdhouses should be unfinished. For proper drainage, the roof should extend at least 3 inches beyond the front of the house. Flat-roofed houses should have a 1/8-inch-deep drip line parallel to the face. Put 3/8-inch holes in each corner of the floor. The box shouldn't be too flimsy—the heat in a thin-walled box can kill young birds. Wrens that nest in milk-carton or tailpipe birdhouses and other similarly weird places may have such a problem.

Exterior-grade plywood or 3/4-inch cedar is the best birdhouse wood; it lasts a long time. Some books recommend PVC pipe, but they're in error; it, too, heats up quickly. Coffee cans and plastic jugs are also poor choices. Metal and plastic usually aren't good because of heat buildup, but there are two exceptions. Aluminum martin houses are less likely to topple than heavier wooden ones, and metal wood duck houses offer protection against raccoons.

Most public libraries have plenty of books that give straightforward, acceptable directions for building serviceable birdhouses. Beware those books that have complicated plans and cutesy designs; it may be assumed that such accommodations are designed with humans, not birds, in mind. I've seen books that specialize in brightly colored, heavily decorated birdhouses, intended apparently to appeal to the pride of the woodworker. One book I studied actually had a birdhouse designed to look like a miniature outhouse.

Ornithologists have discovered that artificial nest structures are useful for birds other than cavity-nesters. Ospreys, eagles, cormorants, and owls accept platforms; terns, loons, ducks, and geese accept artificial floating platforms. Snail kites, which are an endangered species, accept metal baskets constructed for them, and seem to prefer them to building in marsh vegetation.

You and the Nest

*Female orchard oriole
selects site for her nest.*

As far as observing active nests is concerned, our respect for the serious business of reproduction should monitor our curiosity. There's no denying the pleasure of watching the procedure from the beginning of nest building to the first flight of the fledglings. That, after all, is one of the reasons we put effort into erecting birdhouses on our property or landscaping it to attract birds. Birds that nest close to houses are unlikely to find discreet interest in their activities annoying, but "discreet" doesn't include handling nests, eggs, or the young. If a parent bird arrives on the scene, it's prudent to retire politely.

Too much attention to a nest may attract the attention of nest predators, including our pets. Birds that nest farther from human habitation are likely to resent our presence (red-winged blackbirds will attack snoopers). In addition, people being nearby may prevent a parent bird from returning to a nest to care for the young. A pair of eagles in Norway circled their eyrie for days because campers too close for comfort frightened them. The eaglets died from hunger as a result.

It's pleasant that many of the qualities that appeal to us in our gardens appeal to birds, too. What's maybe even more reassuring is that a measure of untidiness is welcome to them. If flowers or herbs go to seed, you can bet that some bird will enjoy them. When you don't get around to deadheading the ornamentals or drying the herbs, you can always announce loudly that you wouldn't dream of depriving the birds of a food source.

HABITAT REQUIREMENTS

Bird	Food
Common loon	Fish, amphibians, insects, aquatic plants
Great blue heron	Insects, fish, amphibians
Cattle egret	Insects, reptiles, amphibians, crustaceans
Green-backed heron	Small fish, crustaceans, insects
Mute swan	Crustaceans, insects
Canada goose	Grasses, marsh plants, aquatic plants, grains
Mallard	Seeds, leaves
Wood duck	Acorns, insects
Turkey vulture	Carrion
Black vulture	Carrion
Red-tailed hawk	Small mammals, amphibians, reptiles, nestlings, insects
Golden eagle	Small to medium-size mammals, fish, reptiles, carrion
Bald eagle	Fish, small to medium-size mammals
Northern harrier	Small mammals and birds
Osprey	Fish
Peregrine falcon	Small to large birds
American kestrel	Insects, small mammals, reptiles, amphibians, birds

HABITAT REQUIREMENTS (continued)

Bird Nesting Material	Remarks
Rushes, grass, twigs, reeds	Likes small wooded islands, privacy
Sticks	Colonial; nests in swamp trees
Sticks	Nests in bushes or trees, not necessarily near water; singly or in small colonies
Sticks	Colonial; tree nester
Sticks, roots, trash	Nests on small islet in shallow marshy margin of pond or on bank near water
Sticks, reeds, grass, down	Nests on ground near water
Reeds, grass, feathers, down	Likes to nest on dry ground in tall grass or alfalfa
Wood chips, down	Cavity-nester; accepts birdboxes
None	Ground-nester, preferably in gravel or sawdust
None	Ground-nester; both parents incubate
Twigs	Builds on rock ledges, in trees, in open situation; may use same nest repeatedly
Sticks, grass	Nests in high tree or on cliff
Sticks, branches, grass, moss, sod, weeds	Enormous eyrie, usually built in fork of giant tree
Grass, reeds	Ground-nester
Sticks, bark, sod, grass	Loose colonies; likes trees and poles, high or low
None	Nests in scrape on ground or appropriates nest of buzzard, raven, eagle
None	Cavity-nester; accepts birdboxes

HABITAT REQUIREMENTS

Bird	Food
Spruce grouse	Buds and needles of conifers, berries, insects
Ruffed grouse	Seeds, insects, fruits
Sharp-tailed grouse	Vegetation, insects
Bobwhite	Vegetation, seeds, insects
California quail	Insects, grains, berries, fruits
Gambel's quail	Insects, grains, berries, fruits
Ring-necked pheasant	Grains, seeds, vegetation
Turkey	Acorns, berries, plants, insects
Killdeer	Insects
American woodcock	Earthworms, larvae of insects
Spotted sandpiper	Insects
Herring gull	Carrion, garbage, marine animals
Rock dove	Seeds, grains, handouts
Mourning dove	Seeds, grains
Common ground dove	Seeds, grains, berries
Yellow-billed cuckoo	Insects, wild fruits
Black-billed cuckoo	Insects, fleshy fruits
Roadrunner	Reptiles, rodents, insects
Barn-owl	Mice
Screech owl	Small rodents and insects
Great horned owl	Small mammals, birds, reptiles

Bird Nesting Material	Remarks
Dry twigs, leaves, moss, grass	Ground-nester; prefers site under low conifer branch
Leaves, pine needles	Nests in a hollow under log or at base of tree, in woods
Grass, feathers	Nests in hollow in ground
Weeds, grass	Nests in hollow in grass
Grass	Nests in slight hollow under brush heaps, beside a rock, sometimes in gardens
Grass, feathers	Nests in scrape at base of shrub
Weeds, grass, leaves	Ground-nester
Dead leaves	Ground-nester
None	Nests in open, on ground or on roofs, on pebbles, wood chips, grass
Dead leaves, twigs, pine needles	Nests on ground, not concealed
Grass, leaves, weed stems	Saucer-shaped nest on ground, near water
Grass, seaweed, shells, feathers	Nests in sandy area, on ground
Twigs, grass, straw, debris	Male gathers materials, female builds
Twigs	Nests on ground or in tree
Twigs, pine needles, rootlets, grass	Nests on ground or above
Twigs	Nests 4 to 10 feet from ground; likes thickets
Twigs	Nests in second growth in shrubs
Twigs	Nests in cactus, mesquite
None	Accepts birdboxes
None	Accepts birdboxes; lays eggs on leaves or any rubble in cavity
None	Often uses deserted hawk or crow's nest.or lays eggs on ground amidst old bones, skulls, fur, etc.; deep woods

HABITAT REQUIREMENTS

Bird	Food
Saw-whet owl	Small mammals, insects
Whip-poor-will	Flying insects
Common nighthawk	Flying insects
Chimney swift	Flying insects
White-throated swift	Flying insects
Ruby-throated hummingbird	Nectar, small insects, sap
Black-chinned hummingbird	Nectar, small insects
Anna's hummingbird	Small insects, nectar
Rufous hummingbird	Nectar, insects
Allen's hummingbird	Nectar, small insects
Belted kingfisher	Fish, crayfish, insects
Northern flicker	Ants, other insects, wild fruits
Red-shafted flicker	Ants, berries, acorns
Pileated woodpecker	Larvae and adults of carpenter ants and other insects, wild fruits, acorns, beechnuts
Red-bellied woodpecker	Insects, mast, corn, wild fruits
Red-headed woodpecker	Insects, acorns, wild fruits
Gila woodpecker	Flying insects, ants, berries, corn
Lewis' woodpecker	Sap, insects
Yellow-bellied sapsucker	Sap, insects, fruits, berries
Hairy woodpecker	Adult and larval beetles, ants, fruits, nuts, corn
Downy woodpecker	Insects

Bird Nesting Material	Remarks
None	Uses woodpecker or squirrel holes; accepts birdboxes
None	Lays eggs on dead leaves on ground
None	Nests on bare ground, flat roofs
Twigs	Will repair and use old nests
Twigs	Nests on dry cliffs
Lichens, bud scales, plant down, spider silk	Nest the size of eyecup
Bud scales, leaves, plant down, spiderwebs	Nest looks like a little yellow sponge
Lichens, moss, feathers, fur	Often builds on branch near or over water
Plant down, vegetable stalks, moss, bark shreds, lichens	Sometimes builds new nest on top of old one
Moss, plant stems and down, lichens, bark shreds, spiderweb	Nests in willows or cottonwoods in arid areas
None	Excavates burrow in bank, near water
Wood chips	Accepts birdboxes
Wood chips	Accepts birdboxes
Wood chips	Excavates new hole for each brood
Wood chips	Excavated nest is gourd shaped
Wood chips	Both parents excavate cavity, in dead or live tree; accepts birdboxes
Wood chips	Nests in cavity in saguaro cactus or cottonwood
Wood chips	Cavity-nester
Wood chips	Cavity-nester
Wood chips	Accepts birdboxes
Wood chips	Accepts birdboxes

HABITAT REQUIREMENTS

Bird	Food
Black-backed woodpecker	Insects
Three-toed woodpecker	Insects
Eastern kingbird	Flying insects, wild fruits
Western kingbird	Flying insects
Eastern phoebe	Flying insects
Say's phoebe	Flying insects
Willow flycatcher	Flying insects
Least flycatcher	Flying insects
Eastern wood-pewee	Insects
Horned lark	Insects, seeds
Violet-green swallow	Flying insects
Tree swallow	Flying insects, berries, seeds
Barn swallow	Insects
Cliff swallow	Flying insects
Purple martin	Flying insects
Gray jay	Omnivorous—insects, fruits, seeds, buds
Blue jay	Omnivorous—seeds, fruits, acorns, young mice, nestlings
Scrub jay	Omnivorous—insects, acorns, young birds
Steller's jay	Omnivorous—acorns, fruits, seeds, berries
Black-billed magpie	Omnivorous—insects, vegetable matter, carrion
Common crow	Omnivorous—grains, insects, carrion

Bird Nesting Material	Remarks
Wood chips	Cavity-nester, tree or pole
Wood chips	Nests in cavity in dead conifer
Weeds, moss, bark, feathers, cloth, string	Nest is poorly constructed, easily destroyed
Twigs, grass	Often nests on human-built structure
Weeds, grass, mud, moss, hair	Accepts nesting platforms; builds on shelf-like projections
Mud, moss, wool	Nests on ledges, bridges, buildings
Shreds of plant materials, grass	Prefers crotch of shrub, near ground
Plant fibers, grass	Nests in upright fork of tree
Plant fibers, lichens	Builds shallow nest on horizontal branch
Grass	Ground-nester
Dry grass, feathers	Accepts birdboxes
Grass, feathers	Accepts birdboxes
Mud, straw	Nests in buildings, bridges, culverts; formerly on cliffs, in caves
Mud	On outside of buildings, on cliffs, bridges
Grass, twigs, bark, paper, leaves, string	Nests in dense colonies; accepts martin houses
Twigs, grass, bark, moss, lichens, plant down, feathers, cocoons, spiderweb	Nests early, late winter, early spring
Twigs, rootlets, paper, rags, string, bark, grass, leaves, feathers	Careless cup-shaped nest in crotch of tree
Twigs, rootlets	Loose colonies of up to six nests
Sticks, mud, grass, rootlets, pine needles	Likes to use platform of old leaves in crotch of tree
Sticks, grass	Colonial nester; prefers willow thickets
Sticks, bark, vegetable fibers, rootlets, grass, feathers, seaweed, cornstalks	Great horned owls sometimes take crows' nests; long-eared owls may use abandoned one

HABITAT REQUIREMENTS

Bird	Food
Clark's nutcracker	Omnivorous—piñon nuts
Black-capped chickadee	Insects, seeds, fruits
Carolina chickadee	Insects, seeds, fruits
Mountain chickadee	Insects, seeds, berries
Boreal chickadee	Insects, seeds, berries
Tufted titmouse	Insects, seeds, mast, fruits
Plain titmouse	Insects, acorns, berries
Bushtit	Insects and larvae
White-breasted nuthatch	Insects, seeds, fruits, mast
Red-breasted nuthatch	Insects, seeds
Brown-headed nuthatch	Insects, pine seeds
Pygmy nuthatch	Insects
Brown creeper	Insects, insect and spider eggs and larvae
House wren	Insects
Winter wren	Insects
Bewick's wren	Insects
Carolina wren	Insects
Mockingbird	Insects, fruits, berries, seeds

Bird Nesting Material	Remarks
Twigs, grass	Nests in conifers
Moss, vegetable fibers, cinnamon fern, wool, feathers, hair, fur	Accepts birdboxes
Moss, grass, bark, plant down, feathers, hair, fur	Parent pulls down over eggs when absent from nest; accepts birdboxes
Grass, moss, plant down, bark, rootlets, fur, hair, wool	Cavity-nester in high evergreen forests
Moss, lichens, bark, fern down, feathers, fur	Cavity-nester
Leaves, bark, moss, grass, cotton, wool, feathers, hair, fur, old snakeskins	Accepts birdboxes
Cotton, wool, feathers; anything soft	Accepts birdboxes
Moss, lichens, leaves, spiderwebs	Will nest in city gardens in bush or tree
Bark, grass, twigs, rootlets, feathers, hair	Accepts birdboxes
Wood chips, feathers, grass, rootlets, bark	Accepts birdboxes
Bark shreds, fur, feathers, pine-seed wings, grass, cotton, wool, pine needles	Cavity-nester in pine woods, cypress swamps
Feathers, plant down, wool, fur	Nests behind bark crevices or in cavities, preferably in conifers
Twigs, leaves, grass, bark, moss	Nests under loose flake of bark on tree
Twigs, grass, rootlets, feathers, hair, rubbish	Accepts birdboxes
Sticks, moss	Nests in tangled growth near ground
Bark, assorted rubbish	Crevice-nester; accepts birdboxes
Twigs, grass, leaves	Accepts birdboxes, 10 feet or less from ground
Twigs, leaves, moss, hair, rootlets	Nests in shrubs or trees

HABITAT REQUIREMENTS

Bird	Food
Catbird	Insects, fruits, berries
Brown thrasher	Insects, berries, fruits, grains
California thrasher	Wild fruits, berries, insects
Sage thrasher	Insects, berries, fruits
Robin	Fruits, earthworms, insects
Wood thrush	Insects, fruits
Hermit thrush	Insects, fruits
Swainson's thrush	Insects, wild fruits
Veery	Insects, wild fruits, seeds
Eastern bluebird	Insects, fruits
Western bluebird	Insects, fruits, berries, weed seeds
Mountain bluebird	Insects, fruits
Townsend's solitaire	Flying insects
Blue-gray gnatcatcher	Insects
Golden-crowned kinglet	Insects
Ruby-crowned kinglet	Insects, seeds, fruits
Cedar waxwing	Berries, insects
Loggerhead shrike	Insects, small animals, and birds
Starling	Insects, seeds, fruits, grains
White-eyed vireo	Insects, wild fruits

HABITAT REQUIREMENTS (continued)

Bird Nesting Material	Remarks
Twigs, weeds, leaves, grass, rootlets	Likes to nest in briars, may use same nest for second and third broods
Twigs, dry leaves, grass	Ground-nester; new mate for second brood
Coarse twigs	Nests near ground; nest similar to mockingbird's but larger
Bark strips, twigs, grass	Nests in sagebrush
Twigs, mud, fine grass, animal fur	Will accept nesting platform; will nest on and around house in evergreen and deciduous trees
Grass, leaves, weeds, moss, mud	Likes something white on outer nest wall
Twigs, grass, bark, weeds, ferns, moss, pine needles, rootlets, porcupine hair	Ground-nester in damp, cool woods
Grass, moss, twigs	Nests in spruce
Grass, twigs	Ground-nester
Fine grass	Accepts birdboxes
Grass	Accepts birdboxes
Grass	Accepts birdboxes
Grass, pine needles	Nest well concealed on ground
Plant down, spiderweb, lichens	Nests in tall tree in open woods, gardens
Moss, lichens	Nest is suspended from twig of conifer
Moss, lichens	Nest on, or suspended from, limb of conifer
Grass, twigs, weeds, string, yarn, rootlets	Prefers open woods
Twigs, grass	Nests in dense brush
Mostly grass	Will commandeer birdboxes intended for other species
Leaves, moss, wasp paper, sticks, soft woody fibers	Nests in shrub, often near water

HABITAT REQUIREMENTS

Bird	Food
Yellow-throated vireo	Insects
Red-eyed vireo	Insects
Warbling vireo	Insects
Black-and-white warbler	Insects
Orange-crowned warbler	Insects
Yellow warbler	Insects
Magnolia warbler	Insects
Yellow-rumped warbler	Insects, berries
Yellow-throated warbler	Insects
Palm warbler	Insects, berries
Common yellowthroat	Insects
Yellow-breasted chat	Insects, berries
American redstart	Insects
House sparrow	Insects, seeds, garbage
Bobolink	Insects, seeds
Eastern meadowlark	Insects, seeds, grains
Western meadowlark	Insects, grains
Yellow-headed blackbird	Insects, grains, seeds
Red-winged blackbird	Insects, seeds, grains

Bird Nesting Material	Remarks
Spider silk, lichens, moss, spider egg cases	Nests in shade trees, orchards
Bark, grass, spider egg cases, plant down	Nests on branch 5 to 15 feet high
Moss, bark, grass	Nests in tall trees in gardens, woods edges
Grass, rootlets	Ground-nester, at base of tree, stump, or rock
Grass, rootlets	Nests on ground in shrubs on hillside
Plant fibers	Nests in fork of sapling or shrub in thickets, gardens, farmlands
Twigs, grass	Prefers small conifer in woods edges, gardens
Dried grass, weeds, bark, spiderweb, hair, plant down	Nests in spruce or fir forests or gardens
Twigs, bark strips	Nests in pine, oak, sycamore, in bottomlands
Grass	Nests in moss at foot of tree or shrub, in bogs or on lawns
Grass, leaves, hair	Likes a moist, shrubby area
Grass, leaves	Nests near ground, in thicket
Bark shreds, leaf stalks	Nests in woodlands, swamps, gardens
Grass, straw, weeds, assorted junk	Will commandeer birdboxes intended for other species
Grass, weed stems	Ground-nester in tall grass
Grass, weeds	Ground-nester in pastures, fields, marshes
Grass, weeds	Ground-nester in pastures, fields, marshes
Sedge, grass	Attaches nest to reeds near ground in marsh
Rushes, grass, moss, milkweed fiber	Social nester, in marshy areas; will strike at intruders

HABITAT REQUIREMENTS

Bird	Food
Orchard oriole	Insects, fruits
Northern (Baltimore) oriole	Insects, fruits
Scott's oriole	Nectar, insects, fruits
Brewer's blackbird	Insects, seeds
Common grackle	Insects, fruits, grains
Brown-headed cowbird	Insects, seeds, berries, grains
Western tanager	Insects, fruits, berries
Scarlet tanager	Insects, fruits
Summer tanager	Insects
Cardinal	Seeds, fruits, grains, insects
Rose-breasted grosbeak	Insects, seeds, fruits
Black-headed grosbeak	Insects, fruits
Blue grosbeak	Insects, grains
Indigo bunting	Insects, seeds
Lazuli bunting	Seeds, insects
Painted bunting	Seeds, insects
Dickcissel	Seeds, grains, insects
Evening grosbeak	Buds, fruits, seeds, insects
Purple finch	Seeds, buds, fruits, insects
House finch	Seeds, fruits, insects

HABITAT REQUIREMENTS (continued)

Bird Nesting Material	Remarks
Weeds, fibers, dry grass	Likes a hardwood tree; tendency to colonial nesting
Weed stalks, inner bark, string, plant down, hair	Gourd-shaped nest, 5 inches long
Grass, yucca threads, horsehair, cotton waste, grass	Prefers to nest in yucca, near water
Twigs, bark, mud	Often nests in colonies
Twigs, coarse grass or seaweed, mud, soft grass	Somewhat colonial; sometimes uses osprey nest
None	Parasite
Grass, bark, twigs, hair, rootlets	Fragile nest, saucer shaped
Twigs, rootlets, grass	Small, flimsy, flat cup-shaped nest, preferably on oak limb
Grass, rootlets, leaves, bark, Spanish moss	Shade trees, woodlands
Twigs, leaves, weeds, grass, hair, rootlets	Usually nests within 8 feet of ground
Twigs, weeds, grass	Prefers fork of deciduous tree as nest site
Twigs, plant stems	Nests in bush or tree
Grass, rootlets, snakeskin	Nests in shrub or on low branch
Twigs, grass, weeds, leaves, hair, feathers	May use same nest for five years, repairing as necessary
Grass, leaves	Nests on low branch near water
Twigs, leaves, rootlets, bark, weeds, grass, caterpillar silk, horsehair	Likes to nest in thick foliage near ground
Weeds, grass	Builds large, bulky nest
Twigs, grass, rootlets	Relatively social nester; nests in conifers
Twigs, weeds, grass	Prefers evergreens
Twigs, grass, debris	Will nest anywhere

HABITAT REQUIREMENTS

Bird	Food
Pine siskin	Insects, buds, seeds
American goldfinch	Insects, buds, seeds
Red crossbill	Seeds, especially of conifers, buds, wild fruits
Green-tailed towhee	Seeds, wild fruits, insects
Rufous-sided towhee	Insects, seeds, fruits, mast
Dark-eyed junco	Insects, wild fruits, seeds
Tree sparrow	Seeds
Chipping sparrow	Insects, seeds
Field sparrow	Insects, seeds
White-crowned sparrow	Insects, seeds
White-throated sparrow	Insects, seeds, wild fruits
Golden-crowned sparrow	Seeds
Fox sparrow	Insects, seeds, fruits
Song sparrow	Insects, seeds, fruits

HABITAT REQUIREMENTS (continued)

Bird Nesting Material	Remarks
Twigs, bark, hair, plant down, moss, fur	Conceals nest in evergreen
Vegetable fibers, thistle down	Nests in leafy bushes or trees
Evergreen twigs, moss	Usually nests in conifer
Grass, bark shreds	Nests in underbrush
Leaves, weeds, bark, grass, twigs, ferns, moss, pine needles, grass rootlets	Nests on or near ground
Grass, rootlets, moss, bark shreds, cow or deer hair	Bulky nest on ground; builds new one for second brood
Grass, rootlets, weeds, feathers, hair, fur	Nests in thickets
Twigs, weeds, grass, rootlets, hair	Nests in vines or shrubs
Grass, weeds, rootlets	Ground-nester
Twigs, grass, leaves, rootlets, moss, fur, hair, bark	Ground-nester
Grass, twigs, leaves, moss, rootlets, hair	Ground-nester
Twigs, moss, grass, fine roots	Nests in depression in ground or on tussock
Grass, moss, leaves, bark, weed rootlets, feathers, rootlets	May nest on the ground or up to 12 feet high in bush or tree
Grass, bark, leaves, hair, rootlets	Likes shrubs, high weeds as nest site

6 | THE EGG

THOUGH IT'S PROBABLY superfluous to fall into raptures and rhapsodies on the perfection of Nature and the absolute marvel that an egg is, I must admit that I continue to be amazed by it.

The size of the egg depends upon the size of the bird laying the egg and the development of the bird at hatching time. An infant hatched with down, ready to follow its parent, necessarily requires more nourishment (hence a larger egg) than one born naked and helpless. The largest bird egg known is that of the ostrich. It's 6 to 9 inches long and 5 to 6 inches in diameter. The shell, which is a quarter-inch thick, would hold a dozen to a dozen and a half chicken eggs. The ruby-throated hummingbird, on the other hand, lays eggs the size of a pea, about a half-inch long. The vervair of Haiti and Jamaica lays eggs half that long.

The shape of the egg varies with family. Seabirds usually lay eggs of pyriform shape, presumably to prevent them from rolling off a ledge. Owls often lay spherical eggs. Both shorebirds and bobwhites lay pointed eggs—they can fit more into a nest that way.

The color of the eggs seems to be regulated by the bird's need to foil predators, though it doesn't seem to be of vital importance. Nonetheless, eggs laid in the open tend to be blotched and to have the heaviest pigmentation, whereas cavity-nesters usually lay white eggs. Some naturalists think that at one time all eggs were white. The color sometimes changes during incubation. The large end of the egg comes down the oviduct first and tends to pick up more pigment from the cellular walls.

In speaking of the color of eggs, certain conventions are observed. A background color is listed and the markings specified as blotched, spotted, dotted, splashed, scrawled, streaked, marbled, wreathed, capped, overlaid, or underlaid. Both *wreathing* (a band of another color) and *capping* (one end of a different color) usually occur at the larger end of the egg.

The surface texture of the eggs also varies. Water birds tend to lay rather greasy eggs; some have a pitted surface and others, like those of grebes and cormorants, have a chalky surface. Woodpeckers lay glossy eggs. Passerines generally lay lusterless eggs, one per day, in the morning, until the clutch is complete.

A *clutch* is the number of eggs that comprise a single nesting. The word apparently comes from the Scottish word *cleck*, meaning "to hatch." Some authorities link it to the *cluck* of a hen. If the first clutch laid is destroyed, the second clutch is usually smaller. However, experiments have shown that some female birds will go to great lengths to make sure that there are eggs to incubate. If eggs are removed from a nest, some species continue laying until the "right" number of eggs is in the nest.

A flicker whose eggs were being taken as soon as they were laid produced seventy-one eggs in seventy-three days. Such egg-laying behavior is called *indeterminate*. Some species are called *determinate* layers: the number of eggs they lay seems to be genetically determined. The female lays exactly the same number of eggs whether any are destroyed or not. The sandpiper is one such bird. In indeterminate layers, the number of eggs laid seems to be determined by geographical location of the nest (whether or not it's a difficult environment in which to survive) and even by the amount of food available.

Birders have theorized that smaller numbers of eggs may be produced in some species because the environment in which they live is kinder and chances are greater for the survival of the offspring. Clutches are smaller in the tropics and become larger the farther north a bird breeds. Ducks and gallinaceous birds (chicken-like birds, including quail and grouse) have the largest clutches, from eight to fifteen eggs. (Some ducks will lay in whatever nest is handy; such nests are called dump nests. As many as forty eggs have been found in the nest of a wood duck—which lays only ten to fifteen eggs.) Clutch size also varies from year to year within the same species, depending on available food. Both the number of eggs and the number of clutches seem to correspond to the security of the bird in its normal environment and to its lifespan.

The Incubation Period

Eggs consist mainly of food on which a fertilized cell feeds. An unfertilized egg is rare among wild birds. (Although an egg sometimes remains in the nest after the others have hatched, it is more likely to contain a dead embryo than to be infertile.) Eggs start their development in the oviduct and stop it when air hits them. When incubation begins, development resumes; most eggs can probably remain alive without incubation for three or four weeks. The development of the embryo in the egg is rapid. The vascular system

Baby bird coming out of shell.

develops first, and breathing begins a day or two before hatching, respiration occurring through the porous shell. The egg becomes lighter during incubation because of the evaporation of water through the shell. It also becomes more brittle.

In some species, male birds as well as females incubate eggs; in those species in which they do not incubate, the males often protect or feed the female. (Some females leave the nest to feed, the frequency varying with the species.) A female spotted sandpiper lays four eggs and leaves them for the male to incubate for three weeks while she hunts up another male and lays a second batch. That accomplished, off she goes in search of still another mate. She may lay up to five clutches per season. This behavior, found also among phalaropes and several other shorebirds, is thought to be the result of their high rate of nest predation.

The prize for the most interesting of all incubating behaviors goes to the male emperor penguin. The female lays her single egg in May and leaves the male to care for it. He places the egg on top of his feet and settles his body over it to keep it warm. Other males cluster with him side by side, incubating their own eggs and helping to keep each other warm in the bitter temperatures. Incubating without food until the egg hatches, he loses about twenty-five pounds, a third of his body weight, during the two-month incubation period. Meantime, the female has been eating as usual; she returns when the chick hatches and joins the other females, who care for the chicks communally. The male presumably goes out to lunch.

Some birds develop bare areas on the ventral, or lower, surface of the body, in which there is a concentration of blood vessels that provides more warmth for the eggs. This is called the *brood patch*, or *incubation patch*. The male of the species, if he incubates, will develop a brood patch, too. Ducks and geese make their own brood patches by pulling the down from their bodies—which also serves to line the nest and cover the eggs when the parent is absent. In those species in which no brood patch appears, the bird fluffs out its feathers so that the egg is next to the skin. During incubation, the bird turns the eggs with its bill each time it enters the nest to incubate.

The length of incubation varies. As with the size of the egg, it correlates with the size of the bird and the development of the hatchling. Basically, there are two types of hatchlings, *precocial* and *altricial*. Precocial birds are those that are covered with down at hatching and can leave the nest the day they hatch. Such birds have a longer incubation period than altricial birds, which are naked and blind at birth. Cold weather can delay hatching a day or more, in both precocial and altricial birds. Most birds wait until all the eggs are laid before beginning incubation. Those species that begin incubation as soon as the first egg is laid have hatching at different times.

Noises may be heard from within the shells of some birds a day or so before hatching; interestingly, the noises cease instantly if the parents sound an alarm note. Hatching may take anywhere from several hours up to forty-eight hours. Water and game bird eggs usually hatch all at once, passerine eggs within a single day. As the time of hatching approaches, the parent birds become obviously excited.

Ordinarily, the parents don't help out in the hatching process. Their help could rupture blood vessels. The baby within has special tools for getting out of the shell. One is the *egg tooth*, used to pip the shell. This is not actually a tooth, of course, but rather a rough, somewhat horny spike on the tip of the upper mandible. It falls off a few days after hatching. The infant also has what is called a *hatching muscle* on the back of the head and neck, which gives added strength to the egg tooth. It soon disappears, too. In a few species, the parents eat the eggshells after hatching is completed, but most remove them promptly, presumably because of their strong odor.

The Case of the Cowbird

Many bird lovers, otherwise apparently normal human beings, go to pieces at the mention of cowbirds. (Often they also lose their composure at the mention of starlings, house sparrows, grackles, crows, and jays.) Though they swear they're not being anthropomorphic, people make moral judgments on these birds. Like all other members of the animal kingdom except humans, birds are amoral; the concept of morality is not relevant. Cowbirds depositing their eggs in another bird's nest are not being wicked; they are behaving like cowbirds. Success in surviving, not "virtue," is the major motivation in the lives of birds. The issue is the balance of nature, not moral judgment.

The word *parasite* has acquired connotations of evil, and, therefore, terming the cowbird a social parasite conjures up all manner of images of cowbirds playing nasty tricks on less cunning birds. Nonsense. It is merely another way of life, a modification of behavior that has proved beneficial to cowbirds.

I become annoyed when people react in such a way to animals, and yet I confess to more than a little anthropomorphism myself. Like other people, I adjust my standards to suit my prejudices, and my own bias is toward accepting creatures as they are, and marveling at the behavior they exhibit. Though far from a crusader, my interest in defending the habits of other inhabitants of the globe has led me to seek out information on the maligned cowbirds.

There are several kinds of cowbirds, in three genera: *Tangavius*, *Agelaiodes*, and *Molothrus*. Of *Tangavius*, only *T. aeneus*, the red-eyed cowbird, ventures into the United States, in West Texas and Arizona. It commonly parasitizes orioles.

The members of the genus *Agelaiodes*, which has two species and three races, are nonparasitic. They have rounded wings, "female" coloration in both males and females, no known courtship display, and a song unlike that of other cowbirds. *A. badius*, the bay-winged cowbird, usually uses the nests of other birds (occasionally it makes a nest of its own), but incubates the eggs and rears the young itself. These cowbirds are said to be monogamous. Sometimes several females lay in one nest; other times they actually fight for the nest of a particular bird. Their five eggs, nearly round, are a dirty white, freckled grayish or reddish brown. Incubation takes twelve to thirteen days. Note that the bay-winged cowbird is the most primitive of all the cowbirds. Moreover, it has its own parasite, the screaming cowbird, *Molothrus rufo-axillarius*; the young grow up amicably together in the same nest.

This third genus, *Molothrus*, is typical of the cowbirds most of us know; they have pointed wings, and the male has darker plumage than the female. They have a courtship display and typical song, and are parasitic. There are three species and ten races. The screaming cowbird is strictly monogamous; the female lays five eggs, which are difficult to distinguish from those of the bay-winged cowbird, although they are usually more reddish than grayish in their freckles. They parasitize only bay-winged cowbirds.

One species of *Molothrus* that I find rather charming is the shiny cowbird, *M. bonariensis*, which tries to build a nest but apparently can't remember how it's done. Shiny cowbirds waste a lot of eggs as a result of being such klutzes; frequently they drop eggs on the ground. Sometimes they lay eggs in old abandoned nests or in nests where incubation is so far along that there is no opportunity for their eggs to hatch. Sometimes so many females lay eggs in a single nest that incubation is impossible. Incubation takes over eleven days, and it is estimated that a single female may lay sixty to one hundred eggs, which show great variety in size, color, and markings. (Maybe somebody should domesticate them and develop a market for shiny cowbird eggs!) Shiny cowbirds are chiefly monogamous and, though parasitic, not terribly effective parasites—ornithologists consider them to be in an early and imperfect stage of parasitism. They seem to be fascinated by nestboxes and the domed nests of ovenbirds, but afraid to enter them. They are partial to mockingbirds and yellow-breasted marsh birds as hosts, but use the nests of many other small passerines, too.

It's the brown-headed cowbird, or North American cowbird, *M. ater*, that's common in North America. This species uses the nests of *195* other species. These cowbirds migrate and are considered polygamous, the male more so than the female. Normally the female lays five eggs (but one raiser of fledglings reported fourteen eggs), and the incubation period is ten days, which is generally shorter than the incubation period of its host. The brown-headed cowbird is not specific in its parasitism but always chooses nests in which the host eggs are smaller than its own. The female lays four to six white eggs splotched with brown, not all in the same nest. (Occasionally its eggs are found in an unsuitable nest, that is, one in which the host would feed the nestling inappropriate food.) The female escapes the attention of the host by depositing her eggs when the incubating bird is absent—often just before dawn.

The cowbird baby is off to a head start over the babies of the bird rearing it. It doubles in weight the first day after hatching and begins to open its eyes on the fourth day (getting them fully open on the fifth day). On the fifth day feathers appear, and the cowbird has greatly increased in size and weight. Cowbird nestlings and fledglings probably eat a larger variety of food than any other young bird. The cowbird needs only ten days as a nestling, but follows and begs from its "parents" for two or three weeks after leaving the nest. A tiny ruby-crowned kinglet has been observed feeding a fledgling cowbird; so have Grace's warblers and golden-cheeked warblers.

Whereas nestlings of nonparasitic birds crouch down and remain quiet if a stranger approaches the nest, cowbird youngsters beg from everybody and anybody. They beg from their foster parents for a few weeks, and then beg from other birds. Even after the cowbirds learn to fly, they stay around the nest for a couple of days.

It is not true that cowbirds puncture the eggs of other species. It was Audubon's theory that the foster parents of the cowbird neglected incubating their own eggs while trying to feed the hatchling cowbird. Their own eggs, therefore, became rotten and so both hatchling and parents disposed of them. He said the cowbird hatchlings were unlike those of the European cuckoo, which jostle their foster hatchlings out of the nest. Normally the host is able to fledge some of its own brood.

Not all recipients of cowbird eggs actually rear the young. Of the 195 species in whose nests brown-headed cowbird eggs have been known to be laid, ninety-one have been reported as actual foster parents. Red-eyed vireos sometimes recognize the eggs as alien and remove them from the nest; the yellow warbler always recognizes them and builds another nest on top of one containing a cowbird egg (repeating the procedure as many as eight times to escape the offenders). It is not uncommon to find more than one cowbird egg in a single nest—a mockingbird nest found in San Benito, Texas, for example, contained eight cowbird eggs and two mockingbird eggs. It is assumed that multiple cowbird eggs are the products of several visiting females, not the entire batch of a single bird.

No one is certain how parasitism developed in cowbirds, whether it was an evolutionary process in response to need or the result of a few mutations. One interesting theory of how cowbirds began the practice of depositing eggs in the nests of other birds suggests they couldn't spare the time required for their eggs to incubate in one area since, by trade, they were followers of buffalo. (At one time they were commonly called buffalo birds.) Some ornithologists think they may not have been able to distinguish between an old and a currently inhabited nest, though most birds can. (Of course, most birds build their own nests, too.)

Those who claim that cowbirds are monogamous point out that this behavior suggests they originally cared for their young. Even now, some kinds of cowbirds incubate and brood, but the female loses interest after laying and the male takes over most of the protection of the young. Males in other cowbird species are not protective and have a weakened territorial instinct—and maybe that explains why the female uses foster parents.

ALL ABOUT EGGS

Bird	Shape of Egg	Texture of Shell
common loon	oval	slightly glossy, thick, granular
Canada goose	oval[1]	smooth or slightly rough; thick; dull, not glossy
mallard	long and oval	smooth with little luster
wood duck	oval	smooth and glossy
black vulture	oval to long oval	smooth, without gloss
turkey vulture	long oval	smooth or finely granulated
bald eagle	oval to short oval	
osprey	short to long oval	smooth or finely granulated
bobwhite	short and pyriform, quite pointed	smooth, with slight gloss; hard, tough shell
ruffed grouse	short to long oval	smooth, with slight gloss
ring-necked pheasant	oval to short oval	
turkey	short to long oval, sometimes pointed	smooth, with no gloss
killdeer	oval to pyriform and quite pointed	smooth, with no gloss

ALL ABOUT EGGS (continued)

Base Color	Decoration	Who Incubates
greenish or brownish	scattered spots or blotches of brown or black	mostly female
creamy or dirty-looking white or dull yellowish green		female
light greenish or grayish buff to white		female
creamy, dull white, or pale buff		female
gray-green, bluish white, or dull white	large splotches or spots of pale chocolate or lavender wreathed or clustered at the large end and overlaid with dark brown blotches and spots	both parents
dull or creamy white	irregular spots, blotches, and splashes of pale brown with overlay of bright brown	both parents
dull white		both parents
white or pale pink	heavily spotted or blotched with a rich or reddish brown	female
dull or creamy white		both parents[2]
buff	some are specked with brownish spots	female
rich, brownish olive or olive-buff		female
pale buff or buffy white	evenly marked with reddish brown or pinkish buff spots or fine dots	female[3]
buff	bold black or brown spots, scrawls, and blotches; sometimes wreathed or capped	both parents

ALL ABOUT EGGS

Bird	Shape of Egg	Texture of Shell
American woodcock	oval	smooth, with slight gloss
rock dove	oval to elliptical	smooth and glossy
ground dove	oval to elliptical[5]	smooth, with little or no gloss
mourning dove	oval to elliptical	smooth, with slight gloss
barn-owl	elliptical	finely granulated, with little or no gloss
screech owl	elliptical to spherical	finely granulated and glossy
whip-poor-will	oval to elliptical	smooth and glossy
chimney swift	long oval to cylindrical	smooth and glossy
ruby-throated hummingbird (and other hummingbirds that nest north of Mexico)	elliptical[8]	smooth
belted kingfisher	short oval to elliptical	smooth and glossy
northern flicker	oval to short oval	smooth and glossy
downy woodpecker	oval to short oval	smooth, with no gloss
hairy woodpecker	oval to elliptical	smooth and glossy
pileated woodpecker	oval to elliptical, sometimes pointed	smooth and glossy

Base Color	Decoration	Who Incubates
pinkish brown	light brown spots or blotches overlaid with darker brown markings	female[4]
white	none	both parents
white	none	both parents
white	none	both parents
white	none	female[6]
white	none	mostly or exclusively female
white	irregularly spotted and blotched with gray and overlaid with brown	female
white[7]	none	both parents, sometimes simultaneously
white	none	female
white	none	both parents
white	none	normally male at night and both parents take turns during the day[9]
white	none	both parents
white	none	both parents
white	none	both parents

ALL ABOUT EGGS

Bird	Shape of Egg	Texture of Shell
red-headed wood-pecker	oval to short oval	smooth and glossy
eastern kingbird	short to long oval	smooth and glossy
eastern phoebe	oval	smooth, with no gloss
barn swallow	oval to long oval	smooth, with no gloss
tree swallow	oval to long oval	smooth, with no gloss
purple martin	oval to long oval	smooth and slightly glossy
common raven	oval to long oval	slightly rough, with no gloss
crow	oval	slightly rough, with some gloss
blue jay	oval	smooth, with slight gloss
Steller's jay		
scrub jay (Florida and Rocky Mountains)	oval	smooth, with little gloss
Clark's nutcracker		
tufted titmouse	oval to long oval	smooth, without gloss
black-capped chickadee and Carolina chickadee	oval to short oval	smooth, with little gloss; thin shell
brown creeper	oval to short oval[11]	smooth, without gloss

ALL ABOUT EGGS (continued)

Base Color	Decoration	Who Incubates
white	none	both parents
creamy white	heavily and irregularly spotted with brown, black, and lavender; sometimes wreathed	female
white	one or two may be sparsely spotted	female
white	spotted and dotted with brown	both parents
white	none	female
white	none	female
greenish	brown or olive markings in various patterns	female
bluish or grayish green	irregularly blotched and spotted with brown and gray	both parents
olive or buff	dark brown or grayish dots, spots, and blotches	both parents
pale greenish blue	spotted with browns, purple, and olive	both parents
greenish	blotched and spotted with irregular brown or cinnamon markings; wreathed	female
pale greenish	tiny dots of brown or olive	
white or creamy	evenly spaced fine brown dots, especially at the larger end	female or both parents (conflicting sources)
white	spotted and dotted with reddish brown concentrated at larger end	female[10]
white or creamy	finely dotted with reddish brown; sometimes wreathed	both parents

ALL ABOUT EGGS

Bird	Shape of Egg	Texture of Shell
white-breasted nuthatch	oval to short oval	
red-breasted nuthatch		
house wren	oval to short oval	smooth, with slight gloss
Carolina wren		
Bewick's wren		
California thrasher		
brown thrasher		smooth, with slight gloss
catbird	oval to short oval	smooth and glossy
mockingbird	oval	usually smooth with a slight gloss
robin	oval	smooth, with slight luster (turns to a high gloss during incubation)
eastern bluebird	oval	smooth and glossy
cedar waxwing	oval	smooth, with no gloss

Base Color	Decoration	Who Incubates
creamy white	some are heavily marked, especially at the larger end, with reddish brown dots	female[12]
white	reddish brown spots—less heavily marked than eggs of white-breasted nuthatch	mostly female[12]
white	thickly speckled with tiny reddish or cinnamon dots, especially at larger end	female[13]
creamy or pinkish	large reddish brown spots	mostly female
white	fine reddish brown spots	mostly female[12]
light greenish blue	flecked with brown	both parents
whitish with a blue or green tinge	heavily and evenly spotted or dotted with reddish brown	both parents[14]
greenish blue	none	female[15]
bluish green	heavily marked with reddish brown spots and blotches; sometimes wreathed; sometimes paler or darker, perhaps a buffy gray, with yellow, gray, chocolate, and purple spots	female
blue	none	female[16]
bluish, bluish white, or pure white	none	female
pale gray	lightly and irregularly spotted with brown and blotched with brownish gray	female

ALL ABOUT EGGS

Bird	Shape of Egg	Texture of Shell
starling	short to long oval	smooth, with slight gloss
yellow-rumped warbler		
house sparrow	oval to long oval	smooth, with slight gloss
red-winged blackbird	oval	smooth and glossy
northern (Baltimore) oriole	oval	smooth, with slight gloss
orchard oriole		
cowbird	oval	granulated and glossy
common grackle		
scarlet tanager[20]	oval to short oval	smooth and glossy
cardinal	oval	smooth and glossy
rose-breasted grosbeak		
indigo bunting[20]	oval to short oval	smooth, with slight gloss
American goldfinch	oval to short oval	smooth, with little gloss

ALL ABOUT EGGS (continued)

Base Color	Decoration	Who Incubates
pale bluish or greenish white		both parents
white	speckled brown and purple	female
white or greenish white	dotted and spotted with gray	female[17]
pale bluish green	spotted, blotched, marbled, and scrawled with browns, purples, and black, especially at the larger end	female
pale bluish or grayish white	irregularly streaked, scrawled, and blotched with browns, lavender, and black, especially at the larger end	female
bluish white	heavily blotched with brown, purple, and lavender at the larger end	female[18]
white or grayish	evenly dotted with browns, more heavily at the larger end	host bird[19]
pale greenish white or pale yellow-brown	blotched, streaked, and spotted with dark browns and purple	both parents in the East and South; female elsewhere
pale blue or green	irregularly dotted, spotted, and blotched with brown, especially at larger end; sometimes capped	female
grayish blue, or greenish white	dotted, spotted, and blotched with browns, grays, and purples, sometimes heavily	female
bluish green or grayish	spotted and blotched with lilac and brown[21]	both parents
white or pale bluish white		mostly female
		female[12]

85

ALL ABOUT EGGS

Bird	Shape of Egg	Texture of Shell
house finch	oval	smooth, with slight gloss
pine siskin		
rufous-sided towhee	oval to short oval	smooth, with slight gloss
dark-eyed junco	oval	smooth, with slight gloss
clay-colored sparrow and chipping sparrow	oval to short oval	smooth, with slight gloss
song sparrow	oval to short oval	smooth, with slight gloss
white-crowned sparrow		
white-throated sparrow		

KEY
1. 3½ x 2½ inches.
2. Clutches can contain twenty eggs. One nest reported with thirty-seven, but perhaps occupied by two females.
3. Up to twenty eggs have been found in a nest, but may indicate more than one female.
4. Female may abandon nest if disturbed.
5. Two eggs, laid thirty-six hours apart.
6. Female begins incubation at once; eggs hatch at different times, from twenty-one to thirty-four days.
7. Black swift, Vaux's swift, and white-throated swift all lay white eggs.
8. Two pea-sized eggs, laid forty-eight hours apart.
9. Eggs are laid between 5 and 6 a.m.
10. If disturbed at the nest, female fluffs her wings, hissing and swaying like a snake, with her beak open.
11. Similar to chickadee eggs.

ALL ABOUT EGGS (continued)

Base Color	Decoration	Who Incubates
pale bluish green	sparingly spotted and dotted with black	female
pale bluish green	spotted and speckled at the larger end with purple or black	
creamy grayish, or pinkish white	finely and evenly dotted and spotted reddish brown; wreathed or capped at larger end	female[22]
pale bluish white or grayish	dotted, spotted, and occasionally blotched with browns, purple, and gray, especially at larger end[23]	female or both parents (authorities disagree)
pale bluish green	dotted, spotted, blotched, and scrawled with dark brown, black, and purple, especially at the larger end	usually female
greenish white	heavily dotted, spotted, and blotched with reddish brown and purple, sometimes underlaid with gray[23]	female
greenish or bluish white	heavily spotted with reddish or purplish brown, with suggestion of a wreath	female
whitish, bluish, or green	spotted with reddish brown	female

12. Male feeds female.
13. Incubation lasts twelve to fifteen days, usually thirteen days.
14. Female spends three times as many hours on the nest as the male; sometimes they raise a cowbird.
15. Eggs are greener and smaller than robin eggs; catbirds will eject a cowbird egg.
16. Robins will eject a cowbird egg.
17. Twelve- to thirteen-day incubation period; possibly only ten to twelve days.
18. Male feeds female; orchard orioles often nest in same tree with kingbirds.
19. May lay three or four clutches; incubation takes eleven to twelve days.
20. Frequently parasitized by cowbirds.
21. Eggs similar to scarlet tanager eggs, but bigger and more heavily marked; male feeds female when she is sitting.
22. If sufficiently disturbed, female will use trailing-wing tactic to divert attention from the nest.
23. Considerable variation in appearance of eggs.

7 | NESTLINGS AND FLEDGLINGS

ONCE THE EGGS hatch, most bird parents have a tremendous amount of work to do. Providing food for their young can require an almost constant stream of activity, and, in addition, they must keep the nest clean and be on the lookout for intruders. The necessary amount of brooding—keeping the nestlings warm in the nest—depends on circumstances as well as species.

What their parents must actually provide for the nestlings varies widely. In the case of precocial birds—those hatched with down and the ability to walk—the hatchlings find some or all of their own food. These birds feed by scratching for or searching for their food. Altricial birds must wait for the growth of primary wing feathers. For altricial birds, considered less primitive than precocial birds, nest life lasts anywhere from about eight days to about eight months. The time necessary may be influenced by the temperature and available food as well as the size of the bird and its degree of development at hatching. During good weather and with abundant food, nestlings may leave the nest sooner. Prolonged rainfall, however, endangers newly hatched birds because it may chill them or reduce their food supply.

Parents themselves can present a danger to their young, especially among birds whose hatching times are staggered. The first hatched tend to get the attention, and later "extra" ones may be neglected, or even eaten, a practice that occurs among boobies, pelicans, storks, eagles, and owls.

The frequency of feeding nestlings varies with the species. Songbirds may feed their young every half hour or up to forty times in an hour, but the young albatross gets fed only two to five times per week. In general, the smaller the species, the more often it needs feeding, a matter of higher metabolism rates. Passerines may eat the equivalent of half their body weight daily.

Feeding among the birds is interesting to observe. Some birds feed their young from their crops, that sac-like feature found in gallinaceous birds and doves but absent in other families. The crop, where food is stored temporarily before digestion or regurgitation, opens into the gullet, or esophagus. "Pigeon's milk" is the white fatty composition secreted by the walls of the crop. Rosy finches carry food to their young in cheek pouches opening from the mouth. Hummingbirds put their bills into the gullet of the young and more or less inject the food. Some observers say it looks something like surgery in progress. Hawks and owls carry food to their young with their feet.

What with the pressure of keeping those hungry babies fed, territorial male songbirds usually turn their attention from defending the territory to helping feed the young. In some species—notably jays—unmated birds also help out. Interestingly, at first the parents don't seem to recognize their own young (nor do the young recognize them). It's not especially unusual to see a songbird carrying food for its own young give it to the first begging baby it sees, even one of a different species.

Most birds keep their nests sanitary by removing fecal sacs (at first the parents may swallow them), but some are notoriously untidy: phoebes and swallows have dirty nests, and doves, as I have mentioned, are very poor housekeepers.

In an attempt to keep intruders from their eggs or young, many birds use some kind of *distraction behavior*. One method is feigning injury, as the killdeer does. It drags a wing on the ground, trying to draw predators toward itself as it moves away from the nest area. Plovers and grouse use similar tactics. Ground doves, too, fake lameness with dragging wings to lure predators away from the nest. When they consider they are far enough from the nest, they fly. Chickadees and titmice have a "snake display," in which, at the nesting hole, they open their beaks, and partially open their wings, all the while swaying back and forth slowly. Suddenly, they jump upward, hiss, and swat the sides of the cavity with their wings. It is a startling performance, to say the least.

It's possible that parents urge nestlings to leave the nest as early as possible in the hope of foiling predators, at least to the extent that not all the young can be destroyed at one time. If a nestling falls from its nest, by the way, it's okay to put it back. The Audubon Society says that the parents won't abandon offspring just because we've touched them. Cover the nest with your hand until everybody settles down. If the nest itself blows down, try to replace it.

To *fledge* means to grow feathers; when the bird acquires its juvenile plumage or makes its first flight, it is fledged. Fledglings are still quite dependent on their parents and become self-sufficient gradually. The amount of self-feeding or begging that fledglings do depends on how hungry they are. Although you may see fledglings the size of the parent trailing along demanding food, watch closely and you may see that if Mama gives all the tidbits to a sibling, the begging bird will hunt for its own dinner for a while. In time, the parents seem to get bored with the whole business, and the juveniles are on their own.

If you encounter a fledgling that seems to be in distress, the best thing you can do is leave it alone. Despite appearances, the parents are probably nearby and will look after it. You can provide some help by trying to keep dogs and cats away. If you move the fledgling somewhere you consider safer, the handling won't prevent its parents from caring for it, any more than handling a nestling provokes desertion. However, if a bird is truly abandoned (and that's not easy to determine), it needs more than you may be prepared to provide: warmth, protection from direct sun and hard rain, and frequent feeding.

The feeding gets complicated. Make sure you're willing and able to continue, on schedule, before appointing yourself caretaker of a fledgling. If you choose to make that commitment at some point, you can feed an omnivorous bird canned dog food or raw beef kidney, bits of hardboiled egg, earthworms, and fruit, using forceps or a small paintbrush. Seed eaters, however, need earth, charcoal, or crushed seeds to digest seeds. Let the bird get its liquid, by the way, from the food itself. Moisten the food; don't try to put liquid down its throat. Tremendous patience is required and vast amounts of time.

Getting Down to Cases

Canada geese hatchlings are precocial, so they're out of the nest shortly after hatching. Down, however, is not the protection that feathers are, so the parent bird broods the goslings at night and for a few hours during the day. As fledglings, the young depend on the parents only for protection.

Mallards also stay in the nest a day or less; on the second day the ducklings are led to water. The fledgling period lasts for fifty to sixty days. Life is a little more complicated for wood ducks. They have sharp claws that enable them to climb up from the nest to the entrance hole, a distance of 4 to 8 feet. Some observers believe that the female carries the young to water in her bill, but most think the parents coax or urge them to leave the nest and then lead them to water.

American kestrels brood their young for thirty days; both parents have brood patches. The young hatch over a period of three to four days. By the ninth day, the female broods only at night. Until that time, the male brings all the food, but then the female largely takes over the job. The fledgling period lasts fourteen days, during which the youngsters are active but still beg from the parents.

Herring gulls also hatch over a period of three days or more. The female broods for the first few days. Both parents feed the young, by regurgitation, for five weeks. The most common predators of both nestlings and fledglings are other gulls.

Mourning doves are devoted parents that brood the young, which are blind, naked, and helpless at hatching, until they are fledged at thirteen to fifteen days. The male broods eight hours a day; the female the rest of the time. The young are fed on pigeon's milk by both parents; they close their beaks on that of the nestling and "pump" the secretion into the young bird for a period of fifteen to sixty seconds. Later on they feed seeds, worms, and insects.

Spotted doves begin by feeding pigeon's milk and later partially digested food from the parents' crops, regurgitated. The fledglings eat no unprocessed food until they leave the nest and begin their diet of seeds. Inca doves brood their young for fourteen days, the female from late afternoon until morning, the male from morning to late afternoon. Once the fledglings leave the nest, their parents feed them for a week and then start another brood; the juveniles join a flock of other juveniles.

Rock doves stay in the nest about ten days, fed on pigeon's milk and regurgitation and eventually insects and fruit. They get little or no food from the parents during the fledgling period; though they beg, the results are minimal. Ground doves brood their young for fourteen to sixteen days.

Both chimney swift parents brood the young during the nestling period, which lasts fourteen to nineteen days. Both also feed the young, first on regurgitated insects and later on pellets of insects bound together by the saliva-like substance secreted by the parents' mouths. During the fledgling period of fourteen to eighteen days the young are still dependent on their parents for food and stay near the nest. Eventually they begin to fly out and catch their own meals.

Female rufous hummingbirds have the entire responsibility of building the nest, incubating the eggs, and brooding and feeding the young for a period of about twenty days. Anna's hummingbird and black-chinned hummingbird females brood for twenty-one days; the nestlings are fed tiny insects.

Flicker nestlings make a humming noise while they're in the nest. They are fed by regurgitation. For the first ten days the parents eat the fecal sacs; after that they remove them, dropping them at a distance from the nest. Males brood the young at night; brooding lasts twenty-five to twenty-eight days. As fledglings the flickers may stay with their parents for two or three weeks, still getting food from them.

Red-bellied woodpeckers brood the young for fourteen or fifteen days and so do downy woodpeckers. Their nestlings eat insects at the age of four or five days, but it's likely they're fed by regurgitation before then. The nestlings sound like bees in the nest. Hairy woodpeckers brood the young for three or four weeks and care for the young during the fledgling period.

Female wood duck leading ducklings.

The nestling period of the eastern kingbird is fourteen to seventeen days. For the first few days the female alone feeds them, then both parents do. They carry away the fecal sacs and drop them beneath a perch. The fledgling period lasts for two to three weeks, and the family stays together until migration.

Swallows fly within three weeks of hatching and are skilled flyers as soon as they leave the nest. The parents feed them on insects forced down their throats until they can catch their own on the wing. If bad weather comes (that is, too cold for insects), barn swallows simply leave the nest. When they come back, they pitch out the corpses and start all over again. A single nest of swallows may eat several thousand insects daily. Tree swallows brood their nestlings for the first three days of the three-week nestling period. Both parents feed, and both remove fecal sacs, which they drop in water if possible. The fledgling period lasts two or three weeks.

Because crows begin incubation as soon as the first egg is laid, hatching occurs over a period of days. Parents share both incubation and care of the young. The female broods the young for the first ten days of the five-week nestling period; both parents feed the young. During the fledgling period of about two weeks the young follow the parents and beg.

Jays have interesting domestic habits. The young return from migration and find a place in their parents' flock. Florida scrub jays nest one pair to a scrub oak, and the youngsters have to wait until an adult dies to claim an oak of their own. Until that time, they help their parents with whatever brood they're raising and do not breed. Female blue jays brood their young for the first few days. Both parents feed the young; the male also feeds the female. Steller's jays remain in the nest for eighteen to twenty-one days.

Clark's nutcrackers feed the young by regurgitation. They remain in the nest from eighteen days to four weeks.

During the fifteen to sixteen days of the nestling period, female tufted titmice brood their young, and the male feeds the female while she's on the nest. Both parents feed the young. Carolina and black-capped chickadee parents feed their nestlings for a period of sixteen or seventeen days. The female broods for the first few days, during which time the male feeds her. Fledglings follow their parents for a few weeks, but after about ten days the parents stop feeding them. Eventually the parents drive the young away and the juveniles find themselves a tiny territory and defend it—by singing quite inaccurately. It's thought that mountain chickadees feed their young by regurgitation for the first few days. Chickadees are among the birds that are willing to be hand-fed by humans, but it takes patience on the part of the person trying to feed them.

White-breasted nuthatch young stay in the nest for two weeks, red-breasted nuthatches for three. Bewick's wrens are nestlings for two weeks, fed by both parents. As fledglings they get parental care for two weeks, and then they're on their own. House wrens are nestlings for sixteen or seventeen days and are brooded for the first three days. During that time the male feeds the female, and the female feeds the young. Both parents feed the young after the female stops brooding them, and both carry off fecal sacs. After one or two weeks of feeding the fledglings, the female leaves to start a new brood; the male continues to feed the young of the current brood. Carolina wrens follow the same scenario.

Brown thrasher parents eat the fecal sacs for the first eight days of the eleven-day nestling period and afterward drop them some distance from the nest. Both parents feed the young. The male takes charge during the fledgling period while the female builds a new nest; then he helps her care for the second brood. California thrasher nestlings are fed by regurgitation for the first three of their twelve- to fourteen-day stay in the nest.

Catbird females brood their young for the first few days. Both parents feed the young; both eat the fecal sacs for the first half of the nine- to sixteen-day nestling period and take them away from the nest for the second half. Fledglings perch near the nest for the first few days and are fed by the parents. Sometimes the male alone feeds them while the female starts a new family. Both mockingbird parents feed the nestlings for about twelve days; the fledgling period lasts two to four weeks.

Killdeer dragging wing.

Robin nestlings usually remain in the nest about thirteen days, though the nestling period may range from nine to sixteen days. Both parents feed the young; both use the drooping-wing tactic to deter people from approaching the nest. They swallow the fecal sacs. The young birds usually remain in the fledgling stage for about two weeks, but the period may last up to four weeks. Though they continue begging, they are mostly the responsibility of the male because the female starts a second brood, sometimes building a new nest (perhaps on top of the old one), sometimes refurbishing the old nest. They gather in large flocks after breeding and engage in the pleasures of mobbing crows.

The female wood thrush, which has a blood-red brood patch, broods her nestlings alone. Both parents feed the young during the twelve- to thirteen-day nestling period, swallowing or removing the fecal sacs. Fledglings beg for food for as long as thirty-two days. The hermit thrush is sometimes foster parent to a cowbird. The nestling period is usually twelve to thirteen days, and there may be one to three broods.

Eastern bluebirds, which raise two or three broods annually, feed their nestlings insects for two weeks or so. All bluebirds have exceptional eyesight and usually hunt from a perch. The mountain bluebird hovers like a hummingbird while hunting.

The young of shrikes fly at fifteen days. Before that, the female broods them and the male hunts insects for them. Adult loggerhead shrikes impale their victims on thorns or barbs, or sometimes wedge them into crevices to tear apart at their leisure. They kill vertebrates by snapping the backs of their necks, and because of their hunting methods can prey on small rodents and birds as large as northern mockingbirds.

Nestling starlings are fed by their parents for sixteen to twenty-three days but remain in the fledgling stage only four to eight days. During that period they beg incessantly, managing to look remarkably helpless despite their nearly adult size.

The female red-eyed vireo broods her nestlings until the sixth of the ten days they remain in the nest. She eats the fecal sacs at first and later carries them away. The fledgling stage lasts two or three weeks, during which the family roams in search of food. The nestling stage of yellow-rumped warblers lasts twelve to fourteen days.

Both parents of common yellowthroats, frequently parasitized by cowbirds, feed their nestlings for eight or nine days. Sometimes the male gives the food to the female, which then gives it to the nestlings. The fledgling stage, which lasts two or three weeks, starts before the young can fly. After three days they can fly a little, and after twelve days they're experts. They leave the parents after about twenty days.

Female house sparrows develop brood patches. Both parents feed the young for their fifteen- to seventeen-day nestling stage, and about 60 percent of the time they have help from an unmated bird. The staple of their diet is insects, and at first the young are fed by regurgitation. Their chief predators are crows and jays. The fledgling stage lasts about a week, during which the young beg, accompanying their requests with the wing-quiver tactic.

It is mostly the female red-winged blackbird that cares for the nestlings for their eleven days of nest life. She will wing-flap—one or both wings—at any person who approaches the nest. Both parents feed during the fledgling period, which starts with the nestlings crawling out of the nest to perch nearby. That stage lasts a week to ten days.

Northern (Baltimore) orioles feed insects to their young at first by regurgitation. The nestling period is about two weeks, just as it is for orchard orioles.

Common grackles eat or carry away the fecal sacs of nestlings. The male grackle helps the female feed nestlings for the twelve days they stay in the nest only if he hasn't found a new mate. There's some question of whether there is any fledgling stage at all for grackles; if there is, it's very brief and one or both parents feed the juveniles.

Summer tanagers feed their nestlings for seven to ten days, the male helping. Western tanagers are thirteen to fifteen days in the nestling stage. Cardinal parents feed their young for nine or ten days, eating the fecal sacs for the first four or five days and after that carrying them away. The male watches over the fledglings for about three weeks while the female nests again.

Evening grosbeaks are in the nestling stage for fourteen to sixteen days, the dickcissel for ten to twelve. Both parents of house finch nestlings feed them, for twelve to fourteen days. They feed the fledglings insects and berries.

American goldfinches feed their young regurgitated seeds, the male giving the female food for the nestlings. The nestling period is eleven to fifteen days. During the fledgling period, which lasts up to a month, the male feeds the young directly. The female is usually nesting again.

The rufous-sided towhee stays in the nest ten to twelve days, and the male helps feed the young. The dark-eyed junco young spend twelve days in the nest. Song sparrow parents brood their young for the first five days of their eight- to ten-day nestling period. They feed them insects. The fledgling stage lasts nearly three weeks, for the first week of which the young can't fly well. Both parents feed them at this stage, too, unless the female starts a new brood. In that case the male works alone.

The chipping sparrow is the favorite host of the brown-headed cowbird. Chipping sparrows stay in the nest nine or ten days, as do field sparrows. Fox sparrows have an eleven- to thirteen-day nestling period. White-throated sparrows stay in the nest twelve to fourteen days and are fed by both parents.

That's about it. What we know about the care and feeding of nestlings and fledglings is patchy at best. There's still plenty of information to be gleaned. If you're interested in helping to gather information, get your binoculars and find a good comfortable site for spying.

8 | PREPARING FOR WINTER

ALL OF THIS frantic bird activity is geared to the perpetuation of species; all must be accomplished on a timetable. Not all birds migrate, but all birds in temperate climates must prepare themselves to face the exigencies of the changing seasons. For the young of species that migrate, it's a matter of adequate maturity for making a long trip; for the young of species that wander or are resident in the home range, it's a matter of adequate maturity to get through the winter. Either way, it comes down to feathers. The young of a given breeding season must have time to grow the necessary body feathers to protect their skin from rain and cold, and they must have flight feathers.

Adult birds molt—that is, they shed one batch of feathers and get a new batch. Some of them molt annually, some more often. In most birds molting is not a phenomenon startling to the beholder; in fact, it usually goes unobserved except in a few fairly obvious cases such as mallards, starlings, and American goldfinches.

Mallards have two molts. In early to mid-summer, they lose body feathers (as opposed to flight feathers), which are replaced by *eclipse plumage*, so called because the duck's normally distinctive colorings are temporarily absent. During that period, the males are as inconspicuous as the females they closely resemble. (Since the females don't have distinctive colorings in the first place, they are not candidates for eclipse plumage.) In the late summer mallards have a complete molt.

Starlings molt from July to September, and their molt is as startling as that of the mallards. The new feathers, which have white tips, give them a speckled appearance instead of the iridescent sheen of their breeding plumage. Even their bills change color. Males have bright yellow bills, which turn bluish in the breeding season; the light yellow bill of the female is pinkish during breeding. After the molt, the bills are gray.

American goldfinches have a full molt in the fall, when they exchange their bright yellow breeding plumage for the rather somber grayish plumage of winter. In the spring they have a partial molt, everything but the wings and tail.

Most birds lose flight feathers in pairs, one from each side of the body, so their flight is not affected. In some species, however—ducks, geese, and some other water birds not dependent on flight for their food supply—the molting period is one of some danger because the birds lose all of their flight feathers. The Canada goose is one such bird, confined to ground or water during its annual summer molt.

It was the captain of the *Pinta* who noticed a group of land birds far out at sea and persuaded Columbus to shift his course to the southwest. Had he maintained his original course, Columbus would have landed on the mainland instead of on San Salvador.

Going South

Eighty percent of North America's 645 species of birds move some distance seasonally, including the so-called altitudinal or vertical migration, that is, up and down mountains. No one knows who first observed the seasonal movements of birds, but certainly the phenomenon has always interested bird watchers. Our earliest surviving writings, including the Bible, talk about bird migration. Aristotle mentioned migration but also insisted that some birds that disappeared at the end of summer didn't migrate but went into hiding. Others, he said, transmuted: At the onset of summer, the European robin promptly changed into the European redstart! My favorite explanation of migration is one proposed by an Englishman who said birds flew to the moon (it took sixty days), but since there was nothing to eat there, they went into hibernation.

We can chuckle at the notion of birds hibernating, but certain torpid behavior that mimics hibernation perhaps led people to accept it as a characteristic of some species. A banded whip-poor-will, for example, was found in the same crevice in the mountains of southeastern California during three successive winters, its normal temperature of 106° F depressed to 64°-67° F. Lesser nighthawks and several species of swifts and hummingbirds have been discovered in a similar condition during cold snaps when insects were scarce. The torpid condition conserves energy significantly.

Through the centuries, speculation on migration has continued at a lively rate. Systematized observations, however, appear rather late in our history. In North America, it was not until 1866 that Spencer Fullerton Baird, one of the authors of the five-volume *History of North American Birds*, summarized the data on migration. Bird watchers in Cambridge, Massachusetts, established the American Ornithologists' Union in 1883 and created a committee on migration as one of their first priorities.

During the present century, bird *banding* has become an effective procedure, allowing the records of millions of birds to be analyzed electronically. In banding, a metal ring stamped with date and location is attached to the leg of a captured bird. If that bird is captured again, the band gives birders information on its movements. The practice of banding birds to get an idea of their migratory movements started in 1740 in Europe when Johann Leonhard Frisch, a German, tied red strings to the legs of swallows. Anyone else capturing the swallows would know where they came from. John James Audubon used the procedure on a couple of phoebes in the early part of the nineteenth century. Widespread use of banding, by thousands of birders all over the world, amasses mountains of useful information on the movements of birds.

Not all bird movement, of course, constitutes migration. We may think of migration, simply defined, as a regular seasonal movement of birds between widely separated areas.

Some species, such as cedar waxwings, are considered permanent residents of an area even though they may wander considerably after nesting, following a favorite food supply; this is not considered migration, however. Great horned owls, grouse, and golden eagles can be found most of the time throughout their permanent ranges, though they sometimes shift their territories in order to find adequate food supplies—a sharp-tailed grouse unable to satisfy its appetite in North Dakota may wander west to Montana, for example. A species of Asiatic grouse once moved into western Europe and Great Britain in search of food, later returning to its former range. Nomadic birds in Australia move around strictly according to the food supply. In winter it may be only a matter of moving to a lower altitude in the same area, known as altitudinal migration; every thousand feet lower is the equivalent of going three hundred miles south.

MOLTING PERIODS

Bird	Time of Year
Canada goose	summer
herring gull	March & April*/August & September
rock dove	August & September
chimney swift	late summer/before migration
northern flicker	July to September
hairy woodpecker	June to August
swallow (most)	late summer
crow	summer
blue jay	July & August
black-capped chickadee	July & August
house wren	late summer
mockingbird	late summer
catbird	August
robin	July & August
red-eyed vireo	August & September
common yellowthroat	July & August
house sparrow	late summer
red-winged blackbird**	July to September
common grackle	August & September
song sparrow	August & September

*partial molt — body feathers only
**retreats to marshes to molt

The goshawk and snowy owl, resident in the Arctic, move south whenever their food supply becomes poor. The lemmings that form the bulk of the snowy owl's diet suffer sharp declines in population about every four years, so the owls move southward to prey on other small mammals. The young of many species wander, sometimes extending the range of the species. Even among those birds thought of as migrators, some individuals may remain in or near their breeding areas. Although all bird movements involving considerable distance have characteristics in common with migration, true migration consists of long trips, on schedule, to and from areas that have regular rainy or cold seasons.

We can distinguish *sedentary birds*, which are permanent residents in their habitats; *nomads*, which wander following favorite food supplies; *middle-distance migrants*, which move only as far as they must to ensure a food supply; and *long-distance migrants*. Sedentary birds include game birds, pigeons and doves, some owls, and most woodpeckers. Crows and jays are mainly sedentary, but generally retreat from the northernmost parts of their range in winter. Most jays that actually migrate are the young; the adults usually stay together in a flock as a residential community. Starlings are sedentary in North America (European starlings migrate), and so are the weaver finches, or house sparrows. Some blackbirds are sedentary; some drift southward. Buntings, sparrows, and cardinals may be sedentary or migrants.

Gulls, most owls, waxwings, and some finches are nomadic birds. The kingfisher, if resident in the North during the breeding season, migrates only far enough south to find the open water it needs. Titmice, chickadees, nuthatches, and creepers drift southward, too. If you have them year round, your summer residents may be a different batch from your winter residents. Wrens seldom migrate far. Mockingbirds, catbirds, and thrashers retreat to the South usually. Chats are middle-distance migrants, and so are robins.

Even long-distance migration is not necessarily a nonstop marathon. In western Massachusetts, where I live, we begin watching for the Canada geese right after Labor Day. Our location offers what they like—a small lake a couple of miles up the road, hay meadows, and many fields of silage corn. They drift in slowly, but by mid-October our town is playing host to hundreds of geese. Visitors to the lake feed them bread by hand, but when the geese are foraging in the fields they will not permit a near approach. On water they congregate mostly in one large flock, while their forays to the fields may be in large or small flocks. We see them flying often as they perform their various activities. Once the corn is cut they feed well, flying so low over our house to the field next door that we can see their feathers. They leave at the end of November when the lake begins to freeze.

Divers, pelicans, gannets, cormorants, herons, storks, ducks, geese, swans, and raptors are all migratory. Many shorebirds are migrants. The black-billed and yellow-billed cuckoos are migrants, and the burrowing owl is migratory in the North. Nightjars migrate and so do swifts. Chimney swifts fly north in groups of twenty to thirty, but migrate south by the hundreds. All of our hummingbirds migrate, too. The ruby-throated hummingbird migrates to and from the Yucatán, at an estimated 30 mph. The sexes migrate separately, the male arriving first, and move northward as flowers appear. They fly about 25 feet above land or water.

Flickers and yellow-bellied sapsuckers are migrants. Flycatchers, swallows, and martins migrate, and many thrushes are long-distance migrants. Pipits move south; shrikes retreat irregularly from the northernmost part of their ranges. Most vireos and warblers are long-distance migrants. Orchard orioles leave the North in July, immediately after nesting; northern (Baltimore) orioles don't leave until September or October. Tanagers are long-distance migrants.

Why and How

Though it is widely believed that birds migrate to escape cold weather, they are actually almost perfectly adapted to withstand extremes of temperature. They migrate to ensure a food supply. Some birds, primarily insect eaters, start south immediately after the molt following nesting. Others hang around for the fall crop of grains, berries, and fruits.

The restless movements of birds before migration tend toward the direction of their eventual migration. Most birds travel latitudinally, that is, north to south. Some, however, have longitudinal migrations, from west to east; the evening grosbeaks that nest in northern Minnesota and winter in New England are an example. The common ground dove is mostly a permanent resident in the deep South, but it tends to move seasonally toward the coasts.

Once on their way, the travelers frequently experience difficulties. Though running into human-built structures causes thousands and thousands of deaths, weather-related deaths are far more devastating. Sometimes birds are observed in the grips of "reversed" migration— flying in the wrong direction. Small birds are known to travel at about the speed of the wind, and to migrate downwind. Consequently, if the wind is going in the "wrong" direction, so are the birds. Many birds perish in early snowstorms. Birds traveling along a coast may be blown out to sea. Costly as it is, the semiannual trek proceeds on schedule, a phenomenon freighted with mystery.

It is perhaps misleading to talk about the routes, or flyways, that birds use in migrating. Since birds inhabit the entire continent, it makes sense that they must fly over much of it in order to get to the general vicinity of a flyway. However, in North America, birds follow four major routes in returning to their breeding grounds. Some journey from South Amer-

Radar has also been useful in determining the speeds at which birds travel—most songbirds travel at about 30 mph, hummingbirds and ducks travel at 60 mph, and sandpipers have been clocked at 110 mph during migration.

ica north through California and Texas, distributing themselves to the North and West. Another group migrates primarily along the Pacific Coast. On the other side of the continent, birds travel from the tropics through the West Indies and Florida, north along the coast and west to the central states or north to New England and Canada, often along the Hudson River and over Lake Champlain. The fourth and most important route runs from the Yucatán peninsula across the Gulf of Mexico to the Mississippi Valley and points north.

Young birds making their first trip north do not necessarily return to the exact place where they were hatched, but once birds have nested they are likely to return to the same area again and again. The young of colonial birds *do* tend to return to the area of the colony in which they originated, however. Normally, birds of different ages migrate separately. Later arrivals may not be able to find a suitable habitat in their usual summer range and so they move on. One advantage of this is that whatever the existing food supply is, the birds are spread over a wider territory at any given time, so the young get the energy they need to mature faster.

The migration of some birds is much more conspicuous than that of others. One day it may occur to you that you haven't seen an oriole for at least a week, but it's hard to miss the rowdy congregations of blackbirds that gather in the fall before heading south. The migration of some species is inconspicuous not only because it occurs at night, but also because night flyers travel at a higher altitude than day flyers. Nocturnal migrants, such as thrushes, wrens, warblers (except the yellow-rumped warblers), and sparrows, tend to be relatively weak flyers; by day they feed on the ground or in plants, as usual. Strong flyers that feed on the wing, like swallows, are diurnal, or daytime travelers. One day swarms of them infest the telephone wires; the next day they're gone. Hawks, strong flyers that normally have a large range, also migrate during the day, as do geese and other large birds. Ducks and shorebirds are nocturnal, or show no particular preference.

Perhaps the most remarkable aspect of migration is simply that birds somehow manage to reach their destinations, often after traveling thousands of miles. People, armed with maps and having the additional advantage of road signs, get lost in their own communities all over the country. Theories abound—about the birds if not the confused motorists—but no one has been able to figure out how birds manage their navigation. How do they know where to go? In this century, many carefully controlled studies have investigated the question.

One theory on bird navigation is that birds orient themselves visually by celestial navigation, using the positions of the sun, moon, and stars for guidance. Some experts believe that birds use landmarks. Neither of these methods would work in overcast weather, however. The development of radar has shown that birds have reasonably good orientation under, inside, and between cloud layers. Plenty of other theories have been offered. Many biologists believe that birds use the earth's magnetic field and the mechanical effects of its rotation for orientation in navigation. In support of their idea, they note that birds don't migrate across the Poles. Others think that orientation comes through thermal radiation. Since there is less in the North and more in the South, birds seek increasing or decreasing amounts as they fly, depending on the direction in which they're moving. Homing is another possibility, and the molecular theory postulates that migration is accidental, like the movement of molecules. Bird watchers in planes have noticed some remarkable soaring of birds, as well as exploratory flights, and have postulated that this activity eventually becomes successful migratory behavior, supporting the molecular theory. Considering the distances traversed, however, that kind of probing behavior seems far too time consuming.

There are many theories of migration, supported by studies of such complexity that the ordinary garden-variety bird watcher is left floundering in too much information. Among the newer ideas are genetically influenced orientation, encoding of the route itself at hatching, possession of an "internal clock," and learning from experience (young birds are more apt to go astray). There is also a theory that migration patterns are being altered as our climate slowly changes.

Migration after the breeding season stretches over a long period of time. For birders, it is a time of excitement, a time to see species not often easily observed. It's a poignant time, too. Though some birds disappear virtually unnoticed, the flocking that occurs in late summer and early fall is a sharp reminder to gardeners and lovers of the sun that winter is coming. Even if you enjoy the change of seasons and look forward to the coming of a new one, some atavistic tremor of apprehension accompanies the departure of the migrants. A wedge of geese is exciting and exhilarating whenever one sees it, but in the fall it seems somehow less joyous. Maybe it's partly because it signifies the end of beginnings, a farewell. On the whole, it's simply more pleasant to welcome the travelers back than to see them go.

PAUL E. MEYERS

Young robin, ready to fly.

BARRY L. RUNK, GRANT HEILMAN

Mallard drake courting female.

Common grackle (male) bluffing.

BARRY L. RUNK, GRANT HEILMAN

HAL H. HARRISON, GRANT HEILMAN

Different nesting styles. *Left:* Altamira oriole at elaborate nest. *Below:* Killdeer nesting on bare gravel.

PAUL E. MEYERS

PAUL E. MEYERS

Different nesting styles. *Right:* Cavity-nesting screech owl (in captivty). *Below:* Female cowbird removing egg from nest of chestnut-sided warbler.

HAL H. HARRISON; GRANT HEILMAN

THOMAS A. SCHNEIDER, *f*/STOP PICTURES

Above: Female ruby-throated hummingbird incubating. *Below:* Barn swallow feeding young.

PHILIP ELLIN, POSITIVE IMAGES

PAUL E. MEYERS

Red-winged blackbird chicks.

Scarlet tanager family.

HAL H. HARRISON, GRANT HEILMAN

PAUL E. MEYERS

Family of Canada geese.

PAUL E. MEYERS

Above: Cape May warbler, fall color. *Below:* Red-bellied woodpecker in winter.

THOMAS A. SCHNEIDER, f/STOP PICTURES

PART II

INDIVIDUAL SPECIES AND THEIR NESTING HABITS

24" L

38" L, 70" W

GAVIIDAE—
LOONS

Common Loon
(Gavia immer)

BREEDING RANGE: Alaska and northern Canada south to central Massachusetts, and west to Montana and Washington

WINTER RANGE: Atlantic coast from Newfoundland to the Gulf of Mexico; also winters along Pacific coast south to Mexico

PREFERRED HABITAT: Freshwater lakes

PREFERRED NEST SITE: On bare ground in shoreline vegetation, on a small wooded island, floating bog, or muskrat lodge

CLUTCH SIZE: 1 to 3, usually 2

INCUBATION PERIOD: 28 to 29 days

NESTLING PERIOD: 1 day (precocial)

BROODS PER SEASON: 1

PREFERRED FOOD: Fish, amphibians, insects, aquatic plants

ARDEIDAE—
HERONS AND BITTERNS

Great Blue Heron
(Ardea herodias)

BREEDING RANGE: Southeastern Alaska and southern Canada to Nova Scotia and south to the Gulf of Mexico and Mexico

WINTER RANGE: Massachusetts south along coast, southern United States; also West Coast

PREFERRED HABITAT: Shallow water, marshes, swamps

PREFERRED NEST SITE: Tall tree in swamp or rocky island; colonial

CLUTCH SIZE: 3 to 7, usually 4

INCUBATION PERIOD: 28 days

NESTLING PERIOD: 60 days

BROODS PER SEASON: 1

PREFERRED FOOD: Insects, fish, amphibians

17" L, 37" W

14" L, 25" W

ARDEIDAE—
HERONS AND BITTERNS

Cattle Egret
(Bubulcus ibis)

BREEDING RANGE: Minnesota, Vermont, and New Hampshire south to Florida, Gulf states, Texas and southwest and south; rapidly expanding range northward

WINTER RANGE: North Carolina, south and west

PREFERRED HABITAT: Wetlands, pastures

PREFERRED NEST SITE: Trees; colonial

CLUTCH SIZE: 2 to 6, usually 4 or 5

INCUBATION PERIOD: 21 to 24 days

NESTLING PERIOD: to 40 days

BROODS PER SEASON: 1

PREFERRED FOOD: Insects, reptiles, amphibians, crustaceans

ARDEIDAE—
HERONS AND BITTERNS

Green-backed Heron
(Butorides striatus)

BREEDING RANGE: Nova Scotia west to Washington, south through central Arizona to Gulf states and Florida, south to Central America

WINTER RANGE: South Carolina and Florida west along Gulf states to central and southern California, south to South America

PREFERRED HABITAT: Fresh and salt water; wetlands

PREFERRED NEST SITE: Tree, shrub, willow thicket, not necessarily near water; solitary or colonial

CLUTCH SIZE: 3 to 9, usually 4 or 5

INCUBATION PERIOD: 19 to 21 days

NESTLING PERIOD: 16 to 17 days

BROODS PER SEASON: 1, occasionally 2

PREFERRED FOOD: Small fish, crustaceans, insects

40" L

16-25" L, 50-68" W

ANATIDAE—
DUCKS, GEESE, AND SWANS

Mute Swan
(Cygnus olor)

BREEDING RANGE: Wild populations established and growing along northeastern coastline from New Hampshire south to Virginia; also northern Michigan, northeast Wisconsin, northeast Illinois, northwest Indiana, and south central Montana

WINTER RANGE: Resident in breeding range

PREFERRED HABITAT: Protected coastal waters with dense aquatic vegetation

PREFERRED NEST SITE: On ground, secluded; sometimes colonial

CLUTCH SIZE: 2 to 11, usually 5 to 7

INCUBATION PERIOD: 35 to 36 days

NESTLING PERIOD: 1 day (precocial)

BROODS PER SEASON: 1

PREFERRED FOOD: Crustaceans, insects

ANATIDAE—
DUCKS, GEESE, AND SWANS

Canada Goose
(Branta canadensis)

BREEDING RANGE: Arctic coast south to South Dakota and the Gulf of St. Lawrence, east to New England, south along the Atlantic coast to North Carolina; Canada except South Ontario and Quebec and U.S. from Arctic coast south to southern U.S. except Vermont, New York, northern Pennsylvania

WINTER RANGE: Southern Great Lakes and Nova Scotia, east to New England to the Gulf of Mexico and Florida and west from southeastern Alaska to California

PREFERRED HABITAT: Ponds, rivers, bays, fields, saltwater marshes

PREFERRED NEST SITE: On the ground, near water

CLUTCH SIZE: 4 to 10, usually 5 or 6

INCUBATION PERIOD: 28 days

NESTLING PERIOD: 1 day (precocial)

BROODS PER SEASON: 1

PREFERRED FOOD: Grasses, marsh plants, aquatic plants, grains

16″ L, 36″ W

13½″ L, 28″ W

ANATIDAE—
DUCKS, GEESE, AND SWANS

Mallard
(Anas platyrhynchos)

BREEDING RANGE: Western North America east to the Great Lakes and New England, south to northern Virginia and west irregularly to New Mexico, Arizona, and California

WINTER RANGE: Western coast of North America east to Massachusetts south along the coast; inland from southern New England west to southeastern Alaska south to southern Mexico; permanent resident in middle part of its range

PREFERRED HABITAT: Edges of lakes, ponds, reservoirs usually; sometimes grasslands and fields far from water

PREFERRED NEST SITE: In tall grass, dry ground

CLUTCH SIZE: 6 to 15, usually 8 to 15

INCUBATION PERIOD: 23 to 30 days, usually 26

NESTLING PERIOD: 1 day or less (precocial)

BROODS PER SEASON: 1

PREFERRED FOOD: Seeds, leaves

ANATIDAE—
DUCKS, GEESE, AND SWANS

Wood Duck
(Aix sponsa)

BREEDING RANGE: Western coast of North America from southern British Columbia to central California, northern Nova Scotia south to south Florida, west to the midwestern states

WINTER RANGE: Maryland, south to Florida and west to central Texas, coast of Washington south to central Mexico

PREFERRED HABITAT: Wooded swamps, marshes, near bodies of water

PREFERRED NEST SITE: In tree cavity, nestbox

CLUTCH SIZE: 10 to 15, usually 6 to 8 (another source says 6 to 15, usually 9 to 14)

INCUBATION PERIOD: 28 to 31 days (another source says 28 to 37, average 30)

NESTLING PERIOD: 1 day (precocial)

BROODS PER SEASON: 1

PREFERRED FOOD: Acorns, insects

8" L

8½" L

CHARADRIIDAE—
PLOVERS AND TURNSTONES

Killdeer
(Charadrius vociferus)

BREEDING RANGE: Southern Canada and southeast Alaska south to Mexico, coast to coast

WINTER RANGE: Southern New England west to California and north along the Pacific coast to southwest British Columbia, south to South America

PREFERRED HABITAT: Fields, parks, open areas, often close to human habitation and water

PREFERRED NEST SITE: Bare ground, also graveled rooftops

CLUTCH SIZE: 3 to 5, usually 4

INCUBATION PERIOD: 24 to 29 days

NESTLING PERIOD: Less than 1 day (precocial)

BROODS PER SEASON: 1, sometimes 2

PREFERRED FOOD: Insects

SCOLOPACIDAE—
WOODCOCK, SNIPE, AND SANDPIPERS

American Woodcock
(Scolopax minor)

BREEDING RANGE: Southern Newfoundland west to southeastern Manitoba, south to Texas and Florida

WINTER RANGE: Long Island west to the Ohio Valley south to southeastern Texas and Florida

PREFERRED HABITAT: Damp woods, swamps

PREFERRED NEST SITE: Forest floor or field

CLUTCH SIZE: 3 to 5, usually 4

INCUBATION PERIOD: 20 to 21 days

NESTLING PERIOD: Several days (precocial)

BROODS PER SEASON: 1

PREFERRED FOOD: Earthworms, larvae of insects

6¼" L

20" L, 55" W

SCOLOPACIDAE—
WOODCOCK, SNIPE, AND SANDPIPERS

Spotted Sandpiper
(Actitis macularia)

BREEDING RANGE: Alaska and the tree limit in Canada south to California and east to Virginia

WINTER RANGE: South along the Pacific coast of the United States and east along the Gulf states, south to South America

PREFERRED HABITAT: Open land near water

PREFERRED NEST SITE: Depression in the ground, sometimes in colonies

CLUTCH SIZE: 4

INCUBATION PERIOD: 20 to 24 days

NESTLING PERIOD: Less than 1 day (precocial)

BROODS PER SEASON: Probably 1

PREFERRED FOOD: Insects

LARIDAE—
GULLS AND TERNS

Herring Gull
(Larus argentatus)

BREEDING RANGE: Arctic, northern Alaska except North Slope, Mackenzie province, south along Atlantic to South Carolina; Pacific coast to central British Columbia and larger inland lakes to Minnesota

WINTER RANGE: Newfoundland south and west to Great Lakes, south to Gulf of Mexico; southern Alaska along coast to Mexico

PREFERRED HABITAT: Shores, farmland, dumps

PREFERRED NEST SITE: On ground in open sandy area

CLUTCH SIZE: 2 to 3

INCUBATION PERIOD: 26 days

NESTLING PERIOD: A few days

BROODS PER SEASON: 1

PREFERRED FOOD: Carrion, garbage, marine animals

28" L

25" L

CATHARTIDAE—
AMERICAN VULTURES

Turkey Vulture
(Cathartes aura)

BREEDING RANGE: Southern New England west to the Great Lakes, thence through southern Canada to British Columbia, south to South America

WINTER RANGE: New Jersey and Maryland west through Ohio to southern California and south

PREFERRED HABITAT: Various, including wooded and open, wet and dry

PREFERRED NEST SITE: On the ground, among rocks or gravel; in sawdust in hollow tree trunks

CLUTCH SIZE: 1 to 3, usually 2

INCUBATION PERIOD: 30 to 41 days

NESTLING PERIOD: 70 to 84 days

BROODS PER SEASON: 1

PREFERRED FOOD: Carrion

CATHARTIDAE—
AMERICAN VULTURES

Black Vulture
(Coragyps atratus)

BREEDING RANGE: Mason-Dixon line to Missouri and south through Texas and southern New Mexico and Arizona and south

WINTER RANGE: Permanent resident in most of breeding range

PREFERRED HABITAT: Various

PREFERRED NEST SITE: Hollow stumps, thickets, caves

CLUTCH SIZE: 2

INCUBATION PERIOD: 28 to 29 days

NESTLING PERIOD: 67 to 74 days

BROODS PER SEASON: 1

PREFERRED FOOD: Carrion

18″ L, 48″ W

32″ L, 78″ W

ACCIPITRIDAE—
KITES, HAWKS, AND EAGLES

Red-tailed Hawk
(Buteo jamaicensis)

BREEDING RANGE: Central Quebec west to Alaska and the Yukon, south to Mexico and Florida

WINTER RANGE: Central New England west to southwestern British Columbia, south

PREFERRED HABITAT: Dry wooded or open areas, marshes, deserts

PREFERRED NEST SITE: Forest tree, isolated tree, cliff

CLUTCH SIZE: 1 to 5, usually 2 or 3

INCUBATION PERIOD: 28 days

NESTLING PERIOD: 4 to 5 weeks

BROODS PER SEASON: 1

PREFERRED FOOD: Small mammals, amphibians, reptiles, nestlings, insects

ACCIPITRIDAE—
KITES, HAWKS, AND EAGLES

Golden Eagle
(Aquila chrysaetos)

BREEDING RANGE: Northern Alaska and Yukon, south through the mountains from California to the edges of the Great Plains to Mexico; central and southern Canada

WINTER RANGE: Withdraws from most northern part of range

PREFERRED HABITAT: Open mountains, foothills

PREFERRED NEST SITE: Cliff or large tree

CLUTCH SIZE: 1 to 4, usually 2 or 3

INCUBATION PERIOD: 43 days

NESTLING PERIOD: 12 weeks

BROODS PER SEASON: 1

PREFERRED FOOD: Small to medium-size mammals, fish, reptiles, carrion

32" L, 80" W

16½" L, 42" W

ACCIPITRIDAE—
KITES, HAWKS, AND EAGLES

Bald Eagle
(Haliaeetus leucocephalus)

BREEDING RANGE: Formerly throughout North America; today primarily in Alaska and western Canada, the Great Lakes area, Chesapeake Bay, and southern Florida

WINTER RANGE: Southern Canada west to coastal Alaska and south to southern California and Florida

PREFERRED HABITAT: Near large bodies of water

PREFERRED NEST SITE: In a fork near the top of a giant tree, usually 50 or 60 feet up

CLUTCH SIZE: 1 to 3, usually 2

INCUBATION PERIOD: 35 days

NESTLING PERIOD: 72 to 74 days

BROODS PER SEASON: 1

PREFERRED FOOD: Fish, small to medium-size mammals

ACCIPITRIDAE—
KITES, HAWKS, AND EAGLES

Northern Harrier
(Circus cyaneus)

BREEDING RANGE: Most of North America south to northern Virginia and west to Texas panhandle, California

WINTER RANGE: Nova Scotia, southern New England west to the Pacific and south to South America

PREFERRED HABITAT: Marshes, fields

PREFERRED NEST SITE: On or near the ground

CLUTCH SIZE: 3 to 9, usually 5

INCUBATION PERIOD: 24 days

NESTLING PERIOD: 5 to 6 weeks

BROODS PER SEASON: 1

PREFERRED FOOD: Small mammals and birds

22" L, 54" W

15" L, 40" W

PANDIONIDAE—
OSPREYS

Osprey
(Pandion haliaetus)

BREEDING RANGE: Practically worldwide. In North America: Alaska, Canada south along coast to Florida along Gulf coast to Louisiana; in west, south to north California, New Mexico

WINTER RANGE: Florida and the Gulf states and south, Baja California, southwest Arizona, Mexican coastlines

PREFERRED HABITAT: Near fresh or salt water

PREFERRED NEST SITE: From ground level to as high as 60 feet up, always above surrounding area

CLUTCH SIZE: 2 to 4, usually 3

INCUBATION PERIOD: 28 to 35 days

NESTLING PERIOD: 8 to 10 weeks

BROODS PER SEASON: 1

PREFERRED FOOD: Fish

FALCONIDAE—
FALCONS

Peregrine Falcon
(Falco peregrinus)

BREEDING RANGE: Arctic south to Baja California, east to west Texas; reintroduced in some eastern cities

WINTER RANGE: Washington and western United States south to South America; in east, south from New Jersey to Gulf states and Mexico

PREFERRED HABITAT: Open country, cliffs to city buildings

PREFERRED NEST SITE: High ledge on cliff or building

CLUTCH SIZE: 2 to 7, usually 4

INCUBATION PERIOD: 30 days

NESTLING PERIOD: 5 to 7 weeks

BROODS PER SEASON: 1

PREFERRED FOOD: Small to large birds

11″ L

13″ L

FALCONIDAE—
FALCONS

American Kestrel
(Falco sparverius)

BREEDING RANGE: Nova Scotia west to central Alaska and Northwest Territories, south to Baja California, east to Florida and the Gulf states, South America

WINTER RANGE: Southern Ontario west to British Columbia and south

PREFERRED HABITAT: Open areas, from forest edges to cities

PREFERRED NEST SITE: Cavity in tree, buildings, nestbox

CLUTCH SIZE: 3 to 7, usually 4 or 5

INCUBATION PERIOD: 29 to 31 days

NESTLING PERIOD: 30 to 31 days

PREFERRED FOOD: Insects, small mammals, reptiles, amphibians, birds

PHASIANIDAE—
GROUSE AND PTARMIGANS

Spruce Grouse
(Dendragapus canadensis)

BREEDING RANGE: Newfoundland and Labrador west to Alaska, south to northern Washington and western Montana, south central Saskatchewan, northern Great Lakes region and northern New England

WINTER RANGE: Resident in breeding range

PREFERRED HABITAT: Coniferous forests, especially spruce

PREFERRED NEST SITE: On ground in brush piles or under a conifer with low branches

CLUTCH SIZE: 4 to 10, usually 6 to 8

INCUBATION PERIOD: 22 to 25 days

NESTLING PERIOD: Less than 1 day (precocial)

BROODS PER SEASON: 1

PREFERRED FOODS: Buds and needles of conifers, berries, insects

14" L

15" L

PHASIANIDAE—
GROUSE AND PTARMIGANS

Ruffed Grouse
(Bonasa umbellus)

BREEDING RANGE: Newfoundland and southern Labrador west to Alaska, south to northern California, north to southern Manitoba, south in the Appalachians to South Carolina

WINTER RANGE: Resident in breeding range

PREFERRED HABITAT: Woodlands with clearings and second growth

PREFERRED NEST SITE: Under a log, at the base of a tree, in dense undergrowth

CLUTCH SIZE: 8 to 15, usually 9 to 12

INCUBATION PERIOD: 21 to 24 days

NESTLING PERIOD: Less than 1 day (precocial)

BROODS PER SEASON: 1

PREFERRED FOOD: Seeds, insects, fruits

PHASIANIDAE—
GROUSE AND PTARMIGANS

Sharp-tailed Grouse
(Tympanuchus phasianellus)

BREEDING TERRITORY: Alaska and Canada east to western Quebec, south to northern Wisconsin and Nebraska, south to northeastern New Mexico and west to Idaho and Washington east of the Cascades

WINTER RANGE: Resident in breeding range

PREFERRED HABITAT: Open woodlands and brush

PREFERRED NEST SITE: Depression in grass

CLUTCH SIZE: 7 to 15

INCUBATION PERIOD: 21 days

NESTLING PERIOD: Less than 1 day (precocial)

BROODS PER SEASON: 1

PREFERRED FOOD: Vegetation, insects

8" L

8" L

PHASIANIDAE—
GROUSE AND PTARMIGANS

Northern Bobwhite
(Colinus virginianus)

BREEDING RANGE: Eastern Washington; major range southwestern Maine west to South Dakota, south to the Gulf of Mexico and east to the Atlantic; also Washington, Wyoming, eastern Colorado, eastern New Mexico, eastern Mexico

WINTER RANGE: Resident in breeding range

PREFERRED HABITAT: Brush and farming country

PREFERRED NEST SITE: A hollow in the grass

CLUTCH SIZE: 12 to 20, usually 14 to 16

INCUBATION PERIOD: 23 to 24 days

NESTLING PERIOD: 1 day or less (precocial)

BROODS PER SEASON: Usually 2

PREFERRED FOOD: Vegetation, seeds, insects

PHASIANIDAE—
GROUSE AND PTARMIGANS

California Quail
(Callipepla californica)

BREEDING RANGE: Southern British Columbia to Oregon, California, Baja California; also northern Nevada, central Utah, western Idaho

WINTER RANGE: Permanent resident in breeding range

PREFERRED HABITAT: Edges of woods, brush, parks, farms

PREFERRED NEST SITE: On ground

CLUTCH SIZE: 10 to 17

INCUBATION PERIOD: Unknown

NESTLING PERIOD: Less than 1 day (precocial)

BROODS PER SEASON: 1

PREFERRED FOOD: Insects, grains, berries, fruits

8½" L

PHASIANIDAE—
GROUSE AND PTARMIGANS

Gambel's Quail
(Callipepla gambelii)

BREEDING RANGE: Deserts of southern Nevada and Utah, central Idaho, western Colorado, southeastern California, Arizona, New Mexico, west Texas, northwest Mexico

WINTER RANGE: Permanent resident in breeding range

PREFERRED HABITAT: Thickets near water

PREFERRED NEST SITE: On ground

CLUTCH SIZE: 10 to 16

INCUBATION PERIOD: 21 to 24 days

NESTLING PERIOD: 1 day or less (precocial)

BROODS PER SEASON: 2

PREFERRED FOOD: Insects, grains, berries, fruits

27" L

PHASIANIDAE—
GROUSE AND PTARMIGANS

Ring-necked Pheasant
(Phasianus colchicus)

BREEDING RANGE: Southern New England west to British Columbia, south to southern California, ranging north from New Mexico and east; primarily north of the Mason-Dixon line; stocked in many areas as game bird

WINTER RANGE: Resident in breeding range

PREFERRED HABITAT: Cultivated fields, brushy edges

PREFERRED NEST SITE: On the ground in a natural hollow, in grass or weeds

CLUTCH SIZE: 6 to 15, usually 10 to 12

INCUBATION PERIOD: 23 to 25 days

NESTLING PERIOD: Less than 1 day (precocial)

BROODS PER SEASON: 1 or 2

PREFERRED FOOD: Grains, seeds, vegetation

34″ L

13″ L

PHASIANIDAE—
GROUSE AND PTARMIGANS

Turkey
(Meleagris gallopavo)

BREEDING RANGE: Central and southern New England, south to Florida, the Gulf states and Mexico, north to Colorado and east; reintroduced in much of former range

WINTER RANGE: Resident in breeding range

PREFERRED HABITAT: Open woodlands in hilly or mountainous areas

PREFERRED NEST SITE: Depression in dry ground

CLUTCH SIZE: 8 to 20, usually 10

INCUBATION PERIOD: 28 days

NESTLING PERIOD: 1 day (precocial)

BROODS PER SEASON: 1

PREFERRED FOOD: Acorns, berries, plants, insects

COLUMBIDAE—
PIGEONS AND DOVES

Rock Dove
(Columba livia)

BREEDING RANGE: Throughout temperate North America

WINTER RANGE: Permanent resident throughout its range

PREFERRED HABITAT: Near human habitation

PREFERRED NEST SITE: On ledges, bridges, barns, singly or in colonies

CLUTCH SIZE: 1 to 2, usually 2

INCUBATION PERIOD: 17 to 19 days

NESTLING PERIOD: 21 to 28 days

BROODS PER SEASON: 2, 3, or more

PREFERRED FOOD: Seeds, grains, handouts

COLUMBIDAE—
PIGEONS AND DOVES

Mourning Dove
(Zenaidura macroura)

BREEDING RANGE: Southern Canada west to British Columbia, south to the Bahamas and Mexico

WINTER RANGE: Southern Maine west to extreme southwest British Columbia and south to Central America

PREFERRED HABITAT: Open woodland, agricultural and residential areas

PREFERRED NEST SITE: Horizontal branch of conifer, from 10 to 50 feet high

CLUTCH SIZE: 2 to 4, usually 2

INCUBATION PERIOD: 13 to 14 days

NESTLING PERIOD: 12 to 14 days

BROODS PER SEASON: 2 in North, 3 or 4 (occasionally to 6) in South

PREFERRED FOOD: Seeds, grains

COLUMBIDAE—
PIGEONS AND DOVES

Common Ground Dove
(Columbina passerina)

BREEDING RANGE: South Carolina west to California and south to the Florida Keys and Central America

WINTER RANGE: Primarily a resident, but withdraws from northernmost part of range

PREFERRED HABITAT: Open woodlands, agricultural and residential areas

PREFERRED NEST SITE: From ground level to as high as 25 feet, on a horizontal branch

CLUTCH SIZE: 2

INCUBATION PERIOD: 12 to 14 days

NESTLING PERIOD: 14 to 16 days

BROODS PER SEASON: 2, 3, or more

PREFERRED FOOD: Seeds, grains, berries

11" L

11" L

CUCULIDAE—
CUCKOOS, ANIS, AND ROADRUNNERS

Yellow-billed Cuckoo
(Coccyzus americanus)

BREEDING RANGE: New Brunswick west to Nevada and southern California, south to Mexico and east to Florida and the West Indies

WINTER RANGE: South America

PREFERRED HABITAT: Open woods, brush, thickets

PREFERRED NEST SITE: Dense vegetation, bush or small tree

CLUTCH SIZE: 1 to 5, usually 3 or 4

INCUBATION PERIOD: 14 days

NESTLING PERIOD: 7 to 9 days

BROODS PER SEASON: 1

PREFERRED FOOD: Insects, wild fruits

CUCULIDAE—
CUCKOOS, ANIS, AND ROADRUNNERS

Black-billed Cuckoo
(Coccyzus erythropthalmus)

BREEDING RANGE: Prince Edward Island west to southeastern Alberta, south to Oklahoma and east to Mississippi

WINTER RANGE: South America

PREFERRED HABITAT: Open woods, second growth, brush

PREFERRED NEST SITE: Low in shrub or tree in dense growth

CLUTCH SIZE: 2 to 6, usually 2 to 4

INCUBATION PERIOD: 14 days

NESTLING PERIOD: 7 to 9 days

BROODS PER SEASON: 1

PREFERRED FOOD: Insects, fleshy fruits

22" L

14" L, 44" W

CUCULIDAE—
CUCKOOS, ANIS, AND ROADRUNNERS

Roadrunner
(Geococcyx californianus)

BREEDING RANGE: Northern California east to southwest Missouri, western Louisiana, south to Mexico

WINTER RANGE: Permanent resident in breeding range

PREFERRED HABITAT: Open country with scattered cover, deserts

PREFERRED NEST SITE: Bush, cactus, small tree

CLUTCH SIZE: 3 to 8

INCUBATION PERIOD: 18 days

NESTLING PERIOD: Not known

BROODS PER SEASON: 1, sometimes 2

PREFERRED FOOD: Reptiles, rodents, insects

TYTONIDAE—
BARN-OWLS

Common Barn-Owl
(Tyto alba)

BREEDING RANGE: U.S. except Montana, North Dakota, Minnesota, northern Michigan, Maine

WINTER RANGE: Resident in most of breeding range, but retreats from northern parts

PREFERRED HABITAT: Woodlands, farmlands, often near human habitation

PREFERRED NEST SITE: Barns, buildings, birdhouses

CLUTCH SIZE: 3 to 11, usually 5 to 7

INCUBATION PERIOD: 21 to 24 days or 32 to 34 days (depending on source of information)

NESTLING PERIOD: 50 to 60 days

BROODS PER SEASON: 1 or 2

PREFERRED FOOD: Mice

8" L, 22" W

20" L, 55" W

STRIGIDAE—
TYPICAL OWLS

Eastern Screech Owl
(Otus asio)

BREEDING RANGE: Maine, Quebec west to Montana, Wyoming, south to eastern Mexico and Florida

WINTER RANGE: Resident in breeding range

PREFERRED HABITAT: Open woodlands to shade trees

PREFERRED NEST SITE: Natural cavities or abandoned woodpecker holes

CLUTCH SIZE: 2 to 7, typically 4 or 5

INCUBATION PERIOD: 21 to 30 days

NESTLING PERIOD: 30 days

BROODS PER SEASON: 1

PREFERRED FOOD: Small rodents and insects

STRIGIDAE—
TYPICAL OWLS

Great Horned Owl
(Bubo virginianus)

BREEDING RANGE: Arctic to Strait of Magellan

WINTER RANGE: Permanent resident in breeding range

PREFERRED HABITAT: Deep woods to city parks to open fields

PREFERRED NEST SITE: Old nests of large birds, cavities in trees

CLUTCH SIZE: 1 to 3, usually 2

INCUBATION PERIOD: 28 to 35 days

NESTLING PERIOD: 40 to 45 days

BROODS PER SEASON: 1

PREFERRED FOOD: Small mammals, birds, reptiles

7" L, 17" W

9½" L

STRIGIDAE—
TYPICAL OWLS

Northern Saw-whet Owl
(Aegolius acadicus)

BREEDING RANGE: Disjunct breeding range: western U.S., southern British Columbia and southeastern Alaska; northeastern U.S., Appalachian Mountains and southeast Canada

WINTER RANGE: Southern California, Great Plains, Missouri and Arkansas to South Carolina and Maryland

PREFERRED HABITAT: Forests, groves, thickets

PREFERRED NEST SITE: Tree cavities, nestboxes

CLUTCH SIZE: 4 to 7

INCUBATION PERIOD: 21 to 28 days

NESTLING PERIOD: 27 to 34 days

BROODS PER SEASON: 1

PREFERRED FOOD: Small mammals, insects

CAPRIMULGIDAE—
GOATSUCKERS

Whip-poor-will
(Caprimulgus vociferus)

BREEDING RANGE: Nova Scotia west to Minnesota, south to Oklahoma, South Carolina, and mountains of southern New Mexico, southeast Arizona and southwest Texas to Mexico

WINTER RANGE: Florida west to the Gulf states, south to Honduras

PREFERRED HABITAT: Open woods

PREFERRED NEST SITE: No nest; lays eggs on dry ground

CLUTCH SIZE: 2

INCUBATION PERIOD: 19 to 20 days

NESTLING PERIOD: About 15 days

BROODS PER SEASON: 1 or 2

PREFERRED FOOD: Flying insects

9" L, 23" W

5" L, 12½" W

CAPRIMULGIDAE—
GOATSUCKERS

Common Nighthawk
(Chordeiles minor)

BREEDING RANGE: Labrador west to southern Yukon, south to northern Mexico and the Gulf states

WINTER RANGE: South America

PREFERRED HABITAT: Mountains to plains, open woods to cities

PREFERRED NEST SITE: Bare ground, flat graveled roof

CLUTCH SIZE: 1-2, usually 2

INCUBATION PERIOD: 19 days

NESTLING PERIOD: 21 days

BROODS PER SEASON: 1 or 2

PREFERRED FOOD: Flying insects

APODIDAE—
SWIFTS

Chimney Swift
(Chaetura pelagica)

BREEDING RANGE: Eastern North America, from southern Canada south to Florida and the Gulf states

WINTER RANGE: Peru

PREFERRED HABITAT: The sky, near human habitation

PREFERRED NEST SITE: Chimney

CLUTCH SIZE: 3 to 6, usually 4 or 5

INCUBATION PERIOD: 14 to 19 days

BROODS PER SEASON: 1

PREFERRED FOOD: Flying insects

6½″ L, 14″ W

3″ L

♀

♂

APODIDAE—
SWIFTS

White-throated Swift
(Aeronautes saxatalis)

BREEDING RANGE: Southern British Columbia east to western South Dakota, south to New Mexico and west to central California

WINTER RANGE: Southern California, southern Arizona and southern New Mexico south through Mexico

PREFERRED HABITAT: The sky over cliffs, foothills, and adjacent valleys

PREFERRED NEST SITE: Crevices or caves on the sides of steep cliffs

CLUTCH SIZE: 4 to 5

INCUBATION PERIOD: 19 days

NESTLING PERIOD: 14 to 19 days

BROODS PER SEASON: 1

PREFERRED FOOD: Flying insects

TROCHILIDAE—
HUMMINGBIRDS

Ruby-throated Hummingbird
(Archilochus colubris)

BREEDING RANGE: Nova Scotia west to southern Alberta, south to Gulf states and Florida

WINTER RANGE: Mexico, Central America

PREFERRED HABITAT: Mixed woodlands, gardens

PREFERRED NEST SITE: Limb of tree

CLUTCH SIZE: 2

INCUBATION PERIOD: 11 to 16 days

NESTLING PERIOD: 14 to 31 days

BROODS PER SEASON: 1 or 2

PREFERRED FOOD: Nectar, small insects, sap

Between 3 & 3¾ " L

TROCHILIDAE—
HUMMINGBIRDS

Black-chinned Hummingbird
(Archilochus alexandri)

BREEDING RANGE: West of the Rocky Mountains, southern British Columbia and northwestern Montana south to Texas and lower California and northern Mexico

WINTER RANGE: Mexico

PREFERRED HABITAT: Semiarid country near water to semiwooded to suburbs

PREFERRED NEST SITE: Shrub or tree near water

CLUTCH SIZE: 2

INCUBATION PERIOD: 13 to 16 days

NESTLING PERIOD: 21 days

BROODS PER SEASON: 2 or 3

PREFERRED FOOD: Nectar, small insects

3½ " L

TROCHILIDAE—
HUMMINGBIRDS

Anna's Hummingbird
(Calypte anna)

BREEDING RANGE: Southwest British Columbia, western Washington, Oregon, and California to southwestern Arizona and extreme northeastern Mexico

WINTER RANGE: Resident in breeding range but wanders to southeast Arizona, northwest Sonora

PREFERRED HABITAT: Brush, gardens

PREFERRED NEST SITE: Branch of bush or tree, often near or over water

CLUTCH SIZE: 2

INCUBATION PERIOD: 14 to 19 days

NESTLING PERIOD: 21 days

BROODS PER SEASON: 2

PREFERRED FOOD: Small insects, nectar

3½" L

3" L

TROCHILIDAE—
HUMMINGBIRDS

Rufous Hummingbird
(Selasphorus rufus)

BREEDING RANGE: Southeastern Alaska to Alberta, south to western Montana and west to northwestern California

WINTER RANGE: Western and central Mexico

PREFERRED HABITAT: Forest edges, from mountain meadows to lowlands

PREFERRED NEST SITE: Bush or tree

CLUTCH SIZE: 2

INCUBATION PERIOD: 12 to 14 days

NESTLING PERIOD: 20 days

BROODS PER SEASON: 2

PREFERRED FOOD: Nectar, insects

TROCHILIDAE—
HUMMINGBIRDS

Allen's Hummingbird
(Selasphorus sasin)

BREEDING RANGE: Pacific coast, southern Oregon to Ventura County, California

WINTER RANGE: Northwestern New Mexico

PREFERRED HABITAT: Wooded or brush areas, parks, gardens

PREFERRED NEST SITE: Bush or tree, sometimes in colonies

CLUTCH SIZE: 2

INCUBATION PERIOD: 14 to 15 days

NESTLING PERIOD: 21 days

BROODS PER SEASON: 2

PREFERRED FOOD: Nectar, small insects

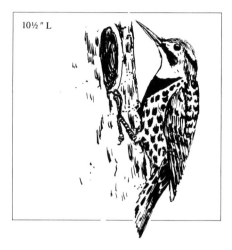

ALCEDINIDAE—
KINGFISHERS

Belted Kingfisher
(Ceryle alcyon)

BREEDING RANGE: Southern Labrador to central Alaska, south to southern California, east to central Texas, Gulf states, Florida

WINTER RANGE: Southeastern Alaska through Oregon, Ohio Valley, southern New England south to South America

PREFERRED HABITAT: Shorelines

PREFERRED NEST SITE: Burrow in riverbank, sandbank

CLUTCH SIZE: 5 to 8, usually 6 or 7

INCUBATION PERIOD: 23 to 24 days

NESTLING PERIOD: 31 to 32 days

BROODS PER SEASON: 1

PREFERRED FOOD: Fish, crayfish, insects

PICIDAE—
WOODPECKERS

Northern Flicker
(Colaptes auratus)

BREEDING RANGE: Entire continent except northernmost Alaska, Keewatin, and northern Quebec; also absent as breeder from central Texas and eastern Mexico

WINTER RANGE: Central New England west to southern British Columbia, south to Mexico and Florida

PREFERRED HABITAT: Woods to suburbs

PREFERRED NEST SITE: Cavity in dead tree

CLUTCH SIZE: 3 to 10, usually 6 to 8

INCUBATION PERIOD: 11 to 12 days

NESTLING PERIOD: 23 days

BROODS PER SEASON: 1

PREFERRED FOOD: Ants, other insects, wild fruits

15″ L

PICIDAE—
WOODPECKERS

Pileated Woodpecker
(Dryocopus pileatus)

BREEDING RANGE: Nova Scotia to southeast Yukon, south to central California, east to Gulf states and Florida (absent from most of western U.S.)

WINTER RANGE: Permanent resident in breeding range

PREFERRED HABITAT: Deep wood to city parks

PREFERRED NEST SITE: Tree cavity

CLUTCH SIZE: 3 to 4

INCUBATION PERIOD: 18 days

NESTLING PERIOD: 26 days

BROODS PER SEASON: 1

PREFERRED FOOD: Larvae and adults of carpenter ants and other insects, wild fruits, acorns, beechnuts

8½″ L

PICIDAE—
WOODPECKERS

Red-bellied Woodpecker
(Melanerpes carolinus)

BREEDING RANGE: New Jersey, New York, Pennsylvania west to southern Minnesota and southeastern South Dakota, south to central Texas, Gulf states, and Florida

WINTER RANGE: Permanent resident in all but northernmost portion of breeding range

PREFERRED HABITAT: Woodlands to towns

PREFERRED NEST SITE: Tree cavity, nesting box

CLUTCH SIZE: 3 to 8, usually 4 or 5

INCUBATION PERIOD: 14 days

NESTLING PERIOD: Not known

BROODS PER SEASON: 1 or 2

PREFERRED FOOD: Insects, mast (not accumulated on the forest floor), corn, wild fruits

7½″ L

PICIDAE—
WOODPECKERS

Red-headed Woodpecker
(Melanerpes erythrocephalus)

BREEDING RANGE: Southern New England west
to southwestern Alberta and central Montana, south
through eastern New Mexico to the Gulf states and
Florida

WINTER RANGE: Migrates from northern and
western parts of range, resident from Pennsylvania
to southern Minnesota and south

PREFERRED HABITAT: Groves, farms, towns

PREFERRED NEST SITE: Cavity in dead tree, utility pole

CLUTCH SIZE: 4 to 7, usually 5

INCUBATION PERIOD: 14 days

NESTLING PERIOD: About 27 days

BROODS PER SEASON: 1 or 2

PREFERRED FOOD: Insects, acorns, wild fruits

8¼″ L

PICIDAE—
WOODPECKERS

Gila Woodpecker
(Melanerpes uropygialis)

BREEDING RANGE: Southeastern California, central Arizona, extreme southwestern New Mexico to
Mexico

WINTER RANGE: Permanent resident in breeding
range

PREFERRED HABITAT: Deserts, river groves,
towns

PREFERRED NEST SITE: Cavity in saguaro or
cottonwood

CLUTCH SIZE: 3 to 5

INCUBATION PERIOD: 14 days

NESTLING PERIOD: Not known

BROODS PER SEASON: 2, perhaps 3

PREFERRED FOOD: Flying insects, ants, berries,
corn

9″ L

9″ L

PICIDAE—
WOODPECKERS

Lewis' Woodpecker
(Melanerpes lewis)

BREEDING RANGE: Central British Columbia through southwestern Alberta and Montana to the Black Hills, south to northern New Mexico and Arizona to central California

WINTER RANGE: Southwestern Oregon to southwest Colorado, south to extreme northwest Mexico

PREFERRED HABITAT: Open woods to suburbs and towns

PREFERRED NEST SITE: Cavity in tree

CLUTCH SIZE: 6 to 8

INCUBATION PERIOD: 14 days

NESTLING PERIOD: 21 days

BROODS PER SEASON: 1

PREFERRED FOOD: Sap, insects

PICIDAE—
WOODPECKERS

Yellow-bellied Sapsucker
(Sphyrapicus varius)

BREEDING RANGE: Newfoundland west to Yukon, south through eastern British Columbia to Nevada, central Arizona and southern New Mexico, east to mountains of Georgia, Virginia, and Massachusetts

WINTER RANGE: New Jersey west to southern California, south to Central America

PREFERRED HABITAT: Woodlands, groves, orchards

PREFERRED NEST SITE: Cavity in tree

CLUTCH SIZE: 4 to 7, usually 5 or 6

INCUBATION PERIOD: 12 to 14 days

NESTLING PERIOD: 24 to 26 days

BROODS PER SEASON: 1

PREFERRED FOOD: Sap, insects, fruits, berries

7½ " L

5¾ " L

PICIDAE—
WOODPECKERS

Hairy Woodpecker
(Picoides villosus)

BREEDING RANGE: Newfoundland west to Alaska, south to California and east to Florida, except arid portions of southwest U.S.

WINTER RANGE: Permanent resident in breeding range

PREFERRED HABITAT: Open woodlands with mature living and dead trees, wooded swamps, residential areas

PREFERRED NEST SITE: Cavity, preferably in living tree

CLUTCH SIZE: 3 to 6, usually 4

INCUBATION PERIOD: 11 to 12 days; 15 days also reported

NESTLING PERIOD: 28 to 30 days

BROODS PER SEASON: 1, 2 in the South

PREFERRED FOOD: Adult and larval beetles, ants, fruits, nuts, corn

PICIDAE—
WOODPECKERS

Downy Woodpecker
(Picoides pubescens)

BREEDING RANGE: Newfoundland west to central Alaska, south to California, northern Arizona and New Mexico, through east Texas to the Gulf and to Florida

WINTER RANGE: Permanent resident in breeding range

PREFERRED HABITAT: Mixed woodlands to suburbs and towns

PREFERRED NEST SITE: Cavity in tree; accepts birdhouse

CLUTCH SIZE: 3 to 6, usually 4 or 5

INCUBATION PERIOD: 12 days

NESTLING PERIOD: 20 to 22 days

BROODS PER SEASON: 1, 2 in the South

PREFERRED FOOD: Insects

8″ L

7½″ L

PICIDAE—
WOODPECKERS

Black-backed Woodpecker
(Picoides arcticus)

BREEDING RANGE: Southern Labrador west to
central Alaska, south to central California, northern
Idaho, western Montana, and Black Hills, northern
Great Lakes and northern New England

WINTER RANGE: Permanent resident in breeding
range; irregular wandering to southern New England,
Long Island Sound, northern New Jersey

PREFERRED HABITAT: Coniferous forests

PREFERRED NEST SITE: Excavated cavity in tree
or pole

CLUTCH SIZE: 2 to 6, usually 4

INCUBATION PERIOD: 14 days

NESTLING PERIOD: Not known

BROODS PER SEASON: 1

PREFERRED FOOD: Insects

PICIDAE—
WOODPECKERS

Three-toed Woodpecker
(Picoides tridactylus)

BREEDING RANGE: Labrador to northern Alaska,
south to mountains of Oregon through Black Hills
and central New Mexico; northern Minnesota and
northern New York to northern New England

WINTER RANGE: Permanent resident in breeding
range

PREFERRED HABITAT: Coniferous woods

PREFERRED NEST SITE: Cavity in dead conifer

CLUTCH SIZE: 4

INCUBATION PERIOD: 14 days

NESTLING PERIOD: Not known

BROODS PER SEASON: 1

PREFERRED FOOD: Insects

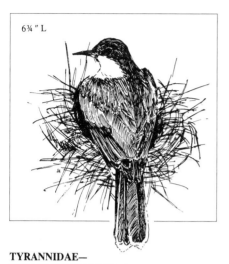

6¾ " L

TYRANNIDAE—
TYRANT FLYCATCHERS

Eastern Kingbird
(Tyrannus tyrannus)

BREEDING RANGE: Nova Scotia west to southeastern Yukon and British Columbia, south through Washington, eastern Oregon, and northern Nevada to Texas panhandle and south to the Gulf states and Florida

WINTER RANGE: Central and South America

PREFERRED HABITAT: Wood edges, farms, roadsides

PREFERRED NEST SITE: Tree, bush, post

CLUTCH SIZE: 3 to 6, usually 3

INCUBATION PERIOD: 12 to 13 days

NESTLING PERIOD: 13 to 17 days

BROODS PER SEASON: 1

PREFERRED FOOD: Flying insects, wild fruits

7" L

TYRANNIDAE—
TYRANT FLYCATCHERS

Western Kingbird
(Tyrannus verticalus)

BREEDING RANGE: Extreme western Wisconsin through southern Manitoba to southern British Columbia, south to northern Mexico and east to east Texas

WINTER RANGE: Northwestern Mexico to Nicaragua

PREFERRED HABITAT: Open country, towns, roadsides

PREFERRED NEST SITE: Horizontal branch, pole, building

CLUTCH SIZE: 3 to 7, usually 4

INCUBATION PERIOD: 12 to 14 days

NESTLING PERIOD: 14 days

BROODS PER SEASON: 1, perhaps 2 in the South

PREFERRED FOOD: Flying insects

TYRANNIDAE—
TYRANT FLYCATCHERS

Eastern Phoebe
(Sayornis phoebe)

BREEDING RANGE: Nova Scotia west to extreme
southeastern Yukon, through central Canada south,
east of the Rockies, to northeastern New Mexico
through central Texas to mountains of central Georgia

WINTER RANGE: Maryland south along Atlantic
coast to Florida, west along coastal Gulf states to
southeastern New Mexico and south to Mexico

PREFERRED HABITAT: Open woodlands, farms,
towns, roadsides

PREFERRED NEST SITE: Ledge, bridge, building

CLUTCH SIZE: 3 to 8, usually 5

INCUBATION PERIOD: 15 to 17 days

NESTLING PERIOD: 15 to 17 days

BROODS PER SEASON: 2

PREFERRED FOOD: Flying insects

TYRANNIDAE—
TYRANT FLYCATCHERS

Say's Phoebe
(Sayornis saya)

BREEDING RANGE: North central Alaska south
through southwestern Manitoba to west Texas and
northern Mexico, west to California

WINTER RANGE: Northern California east to south
central Texas, south to central Mexico

PREFERRED HABITAT: Open arid land, ranches

PREFERRED NEST SITE: Ledge, bridge, building

CLUTCH SIZE: 4 to 7, usually 4 or 5

INCUBATION PERIOD: About 12 days

NESTLING PERIOD: 14 days

BROODS PER SEASON: 2

PREFERRED FOOD: Flying insects

4¾" L

5¼" L

TYRANNIDAE—
TYRANT FLYCATCHERS

Willow Flycatcher
(Empidonax traillii)

BREEDING RANGE: Southern Maine west to southern British Columbia, south to northern California, eastern New Mexico, through Arkansas, West Virginia, and northern Virginia

WINTER RANGE: Central and South America

PREFERRED HABITAT: Thickets, orchards, suburbs

PREFERRED NEST SITE: Ledge, bridge, building

CLUTCH SIZE: 3 to 5, usually 3 or 4

INCUBATION PERIOD: 12 to 15 days

NESTLING PERIOD: 15 to 18 days

BROODS PER SEASON: 1

PREFERRED FOOD: Flying insects

TYRANNIDAE—
TYRANT FLYCATCHERS

Least Flycatcher
(Empidonax minimus)

BREEDING RANGE: Nova Scotia west to southeastern Yukon, south to southeastern British Columbia, southeast to central Wyoming to extreme western Kentucky, northeast to central New Jersey; mountains to northeastern Georgia

WINTER RANGE: Mexico and Central America

PREFERRED HABITAT: Open woodlands, orchards

PREFERRED NEST SITE: Crotch of small tree

CLUTCH SIZE: 3 to 6, usually 3 or 4

INCUBATION PERIOD: 14 days

NESTLING PERIOD: 14 to 16 days

BROODS PER SEASON: 1 or 2

PREFERRED FOOD: Flying insects

5½″ L

TYRANNIDAE—
TYRANT FLYCATCHERS

Eastern Wood-Pewee
(Contopus virens)

BREEDING RANGE: Nova Scotia west to southern Manitoba, south to Texas and Florida

WINTER RANGE: Central and South America

PREFERRED HABITAT: Woodlands, orchards, shade trees

PREFERRED NEST SITE: Branch of large tree

CLUTCH SIZE: 2 to 4, usually 3

INCUBATION PERIOD: 12 to 13 days

NESTLING PERIOD: 15 to 18 days

BROODS PER SEASON: 1, maybe 2

PREFERRED FOOD: Insects

7½″ L

ALAUDIDAE—
LARKS

Horned Lark
(Eremophila alpestris)

BREEDING RANGE: Arctic North America south to northern South America; in east south to North Carolina, northern Georgia, southern Louisiana, south through Texas

WINTER RANGE: Nova Scotia west through Great Lakes region to southern British Columbia, south to Mexico and (rarely) the Gulf states and Florida

PREFERRED HABITAT: Open country: plains, deserts, fields, golf courses, tundra, airports, seashores

PREFERRED NEST SITE: On ground

CLUTCH SIZE: 3 to 5, usually 4

INCUBATION PERIOD: 11 days

NESTLING PERIOD: 10 to 12 days

BROODS PER SEASON: 2

PREFERRED FOOD: Insects, seeds

4¾" L

5" L

Violet-green Swallow
(Tachycineta thalassina)

BREEDING RANGE: Central Alaska southeast to southwestern South Dakota, south to mountains of southern Mexico

WINTER RANGE: Mexico and Central America

PREFERRED HABITAT: Open forests and mountains to ranches and towns

PREFERRED NEST SITE: Cavity in tree, cliff, building, birdhouse

CLUTCH SIZE: 4 to 7, usually 4 or 5

INCUBATION PERIOD: 13 to 14 days

NESTLING PERIOD: To 23 days

BROODS PER SEASON: 1

PREFERRED FOOD: Flying insects

Tree Swallow
(Tachycineta bicolor)

BREEDING RANGE: Labrador to northern Alaska and south to California, northern New Mexico, Mississippi Valley to central Mississippi northeast to Virginia

WINTER RANGE: Coastal areas from Virginia south, along Gulf states to central California, south to Mexico and Central America

PREFERRED HABITAT: Open wooded swamps and near water

PREFERRED NEST SITE: Natural cavity in tree, old woodpecker hole, birdhouse

CLUTCH SIZE: 4 to 7, usually 5 or 6

INCUBATION PERIOD: 13 to 16 days

NESTLING PERIOD: 16 to 24 days

BROODS PER SEASON: 1

PREFERRED FOOD: Flying insects, berries, seeds

6" L

5" L

HIRUNDINIDAE—
SWALLOWS

Barn Swallow
(Hirundo rustica)

BREEDING RANGE: Newfoundland west to south-eastern Alaska, south to Mexico and east to Alabama and the Atlantic; locally in the Gulf states

WINTER RANGE: South America

PREFERRED HABITAT: Farmlands and residential areas

PREFERRED NEST SITE: On, in, or around buildings, often in colonies

CLUTCH SIZE: 4 to 6, usually 4 or 5

INCUBATION PERIOD: 15 days

NESTLING PERIOD: 16 to 23 days

BROODS PER SEASON: 1 or 2

PREFERRED FOOD: Insects

HIRUNDINIDAE—
SWALLOWS

Cliff Swallow
(Hirundo pyrrhonota)

BREEDING RANGE: Newfoundland west to northern Alaska, south to Central America, east to Missouri and Virginia (absent from Gulf states)

WINTER RANGE: South America

PREFERRED HABITAT: Open to semiwooded land, farms, rivers and lakes, villages

PREFERRED NEST SITE: Under bridge, eaves of buildings, cliff; almost always colonial

CLUTCH SIZE: 3 to 6, usually 4 or 5

INCUBATION PERIOD: 15 to 16 days

NESTLING PERIOD: 24 days

BROODS PER SEASON: 1 or 2

PREFERRED FOOD: Flying insects

HIRUNDINIDAE—
SWALLOWS

Purple Martin
(Progne subis)

BREEDING RANGE: Newfoundland west to southern Ontario, west to British Columbia, south to central Texas and east to Florida. Also southwest British Columbia to Mexico

WINTER RANGE: Brazil

PREFERRED HABITAT: farmlands, parks, residential areas near water

PREFERRED NEST SITE: Previously in tree cavities, now almost exclusively in birdhouses; colonial

CLUTCH SIZE: 3 to 8, usually 4 or 5

INCUBATION PERIOD: 15 to 18 days

NESTLING PERIOD: 26 to 31 days

BROODS PER SEASON: 1, usually

PREFERRED FOOD: Flying insects

CORVIDAE—
JAYS, MAGPIES, AND CROWS

Gray Jay
(Perisoreus canadensis)

BREEDING RANGE: Labrador west to northern Alaska, south to northern California, Rockies, and New Mexico; Black Hills; northern Michigan and New York; northern New England

WINTER RANGE: Permanent resident in breeding range, but some wandering south, to Pennsylvania and southern Great Plains

PREFERRED HABITAT: Coniferous forests

PREFERRED NEST SITE: Conifer

CLUTCH SIZE: 2 to 5, usually 3 or 4

INCUBATION PERIOD: 16 to 18 days

NESTLING PERIOD: 15 days

BROODS PER SEASON: 1

PREFERRED FOOD: Omnivorous—insects, fruits, seeds, buds

10″ L

CORVIDAE—
JAYS, MAGPIES, AND CROWS

Blue Jay
(Cyanocitta cristata)

BREEDING RANGE: Newfoundland west to southern Alberta, south to Texas and Florida

WINTER RANGE: Permanent resident in breeding range, except northernmost portions

PREFERRED HABITAT: Woodlands, parks, gardens, cities

PREFERRED NEST SITE: Tree

CLUTCH SIZE: 3 to 7, usually 4 or 5

INCUBATION PERIOD: 17 to 18 days

NESTLING PERIOD: 17 to 21 days

BROODS PER SEASON: 1, 2 in the South

PREFERRED FOOD: Omnivorous—seeds, fruits, acorns, young mice, nestlings

10″ L

CORVIDAE—
JAYS, MAGPIES, AND CROWS

Scrub Jay
(Aphelocoma coerulescens)

BREEDING RANGE: Southwestern Washington south locally west of plains to southern Mexico; central Florida

WINTER RANGE: Permanent resident in breeding range

PREFERRED HABITAT: Brush, river woods, junipers

PREFERRED NEST SITE: Bush or low tree

CLUTCH SIZE: 2 to 6

INCUBATION PERIOD: 16 to 19 days

NESTLING PERIOD: 18 days

BROODS PER SEASON: 1 or 2

PREFERRED FOOD: Omnivorous—insects, acorns, young birds

11″ L

18″ L

CORVIDAE—
JAYS, MAGPIES, AND CROWS

Steller's Jay
(Cyanocitta stelleri)

BREEDING RANGE: Southern Alaska east to southwestern Alberta south through the mountainous regions of western United States south to Nicaragua

WINTER RANGE: Permanent resident in breeding range

PREFERRED HABITAT: Coniferous and pine-oak forests

PREFERRED NEST SITE: Conifer

CLUTCH SIZE: 3 to 5, usually 3 or 4

INCUBATION PERIOD: 16 to 18 days

NESTLING PERIOD: 18 to 21 days

BROODS PER SEASON: 1

PREFERRED FOOD: Omnivorous—acorns, fruits, seeds, berries

CORVIDAE—
JAYS, MAGPIES, AND CROWS

Black-billed Magpie
(Pica pica)

BREEDING RANGE: South and central Alaska to western Ontario, south to northern New Mexico, northwest to Oregon, east central California

WINTER RANGE: Permanent resident in breeding range

PREFERRED HABITAT: Roadsides, thickets, fields, ranches

PREFERRED NEST SITE: Bush or tree, often in scattered colony

CLUTCH SIZE: 6 to 13, usually 7

INCUBATION PERIOD: 16 to 18 days

NESTLING PERIOD: 22 or more days

BROODS PER SEASON: Probably 1

PREFERRED FOOD: Omnivorous—insects, vegetable matter, carrion

17" L

11" L

CORVIDAE—
JAYS, MAGPIES, AND CROWS

Common Crow
(Corvus brachyrhynchos)

BREEDING RANGE: Newfoundland west to British Columbia, south to northern Baja California, northeast through central Arizona and northwestern New Mexico to Oklahoma and south through east Texas to Gulf states and Florida

WINTER RANGE: Mainly south of Canada

PREFERRED HABITAT: Woodlands, farmlands, shores

PREFERRED NEST SITE: Crotch of tree

CLUTCH SIZE: 3 to 9, usually 4 or 5

INCUBATION PERIOD: 18 to 21 days

NESTLING PERIOD: 25 days

BROODS PER SEASON: 1, 2 in the South

PREFERRED FOOD: Omnivorous—grains, insects, carrion

CORVIDAE—
JAYS, MAGPIES, AND CROWS

Clark's Nutcracker
(Nucifraga columbiana)

BREEDING RANGE: High mountains from central British Columbia to Baja California, east to northwest New Mexico, north to the Black Hills; northern Nuevo Léon

WINTER RANGE: Permanent resident in breeding range

PREFERRED HABITAT: High mountains, coniferous forests

PREFERRED NEST SITE: Conifer

CLUTCH SIZE: 2 to 6, usually 2 to 4

INCUBATION PERIOD: 17 to 22 days

NESTLING PERIOD: 18 to 28 days

BROODS PER SEASON: 1, sometimes 2

PREFERRED FOOD: Omnivorous—piñon nuts

PARIDAE—
TITMICE AND CHICKADEES

Black-capped Chickadee
(Parus atricapillus)

BREEDING RANGE: Newfoundland west to central Alaska, south to northern California, southeast to northern New Mexico, northeast to New Jersey; mountains south to Georgia

WINTER RANGE: Permanent resident in breeding range

PREFERRED HABITAT: Mixed and deciduous woods, wood edges, gardens, towns

PREFERRED NEST SITE: Cavity in dead tree or stump, birdhouse

CLUTCH SIZE: 4 to 13, usually 6 to 8

INCUBATION PERIOD: 11 to 13 days

NESTLING PERIOD: 16 days

BROODS PER SEASON: 1 or 2

PREFERRED FOOD: Insects, seeds, fruits

PARIDAE—
TITMICE AND CHICKADEES

Carolina Chickadee
(Parus carolinensis)

BREEDING RANGE: Southern edge of black-capped chickadee range, New Jersey west to Oklahoma, south to the Gulf states and east to Florida

WINTER RANGE: Permanent resident in breeding range

PREFERRED HABITAT: Swamps, woods, residential areas

PREFERRED NEST SITE: Cavity in tree, birdhouse

CLUTCH SIZE: 5 to 8, usually 6

INCUBATION PERIOD: 11 to 13 days

NESTLING PERIOD: 17 days

BROODS PER SEASON: 1

PREFERRED FOOD: Insects, seeds, fruits

4¼" L

PARIDAE—
TITMICE AND CHICKADEES

Mountain Chickadee
(Parus gambeli)

BREEDING RANGE: Southeastern Alaska to southwestern Alberta, south to west Texas and west through southeastern Arizona to northern Baja California; absent from coastal areas

WINTER RANGE: Permanent resident in breeding range

PREFERRED HABITAT: Conifers

PREFERRED NEST SITE: Cavity in tree or stump, birdhouse

CLUTCH SIZE: 5 to 12, usually 7 to 9

INCUBATION PERIOD: 14 days

NESTLING PERIOD: To 21 days

BROODS PER SEASON: 1, often 2

PREFERRED FOOD: Insects, seeds, berries

4¼" L

PARIDAE—
TITMICE AND CHICKADEES

Boreal Chickadee
(Parus hudsonicus) (Brown-capped Chickadee, Acadian Chickadee, Hudsonian Chickadee)

BREEDING RANGE: Labrador west to northwestern Alaska, south to western British Columbia, east to northern New York and Maine

WINTER RANGE: Permanent resident in breeding range; may wander to southeastern New York and southern New Jersey

PREFERRED HABITAT: Coniferous forest

PREFERRED NEST SITE: Cavity in rotting tree or stump

CLUTCH SIZE: 4 to 9, usually 6 or 7

INCUBATION PERIOD: 12 to 14 days

NESTLING PERIOD: 18 days

BROODS PER SEASON: 1

PREFERRED FOOD: Insects, seeds, berries

5½″ L

5″ L

PARIDAE—
TITMICE AND CHICKADEES

Tufted Titmouse
(Parus bicolor)

BREEDING RANGE: Central New England west to northern Nebraska, south to Texas, the Gulf states, and Florida

WINTER RANGE: Permanent resident in breeding range

PREFERRED HABITAT: Swamps, deciduous woodlands, shade trees

PREFERRED NEST SITE: Natural cavity in tree, birdhouse

CLUTCH SIZE: 4 to 8, usually 5 or 6

INCUBATION PERIOD: 12 to 14 days

NESTLING PERIOD: 15 to 18 days

BROODS PER SEASON: 1

PREFERRED FOOD: Insects, seeds, mast, fruits

PARIDAE—
TITMICE AND CHICKADEES

Plain Titmouse
(Parus inornatus)

BREEDING RANGE: Southern Oregon to south central Colorado, south to southern New Mexico and west Texas, west to northern Baja California; southern Baja California

WINTER RANGE: Permanent resident in breeding range

PREFERRED HABITAT: Woods, shade trees

PREFERRED NEST SITE: Cavity in tree, birdhouse

CLUTCH SIZE: 6 to 12, usually 6 to 9

INCUBATION PERIOD: 14 days

NESTLING PERIOD: 16 days

BROODS PER SEASON: Probably 1

PREFERRED FOOD: Insects, acorns, berries

3½" L

5" L

AEGITHALIDAE—
BUSHTITS

Bushtit
(Psaltriparus minimus)

BREEDING RANGE: Southwestern British Columbia along coast to southern Baja California; south central Washington through southern Idaho to eastern Colorado, west Texas to northern Mexico

WINTER RANGE: Permanent resident in breeding range; wanders in winter

PREFERRED HABITAT: Scrub, mixed woods, parks, city gardens

PREFERRED NEST SITE: Bush, tree

CLUTCH SIZE: 5 to 15, usually 5 to 7

INCUBATION PERIOD: 12 days

NESTLING PERIOD: 14 to 15 days

BROODS PER SEASON: 2

PREFERRED FOOD: Insects and larvae

SITTIDAE—
NUTHATCHES

White-breasted Nuthatch
(Sitta carolinensis)

BREEDING RANGE: New Brunswick west to southern British Columbia, south to mountains of Mexico

WINTER RANGE: Permanent resident in breeding range; wanders in winter

PREFERRED HABITAT: Mixed forests to suburbs

PREFERRED NEST SITE: Cavity in tree, birdhouse

CLUTCH SIZE: 4 to 10, usually 8

INCUBATION PERIOD: 12 to 13 days

NESTLING PERIOD: 14 days

BROODS PER SEASON: 1

PREFERRED FOOD: Insects, seeds, fruits, mast

4″ L

3½″ L

SITTIDAE—
NUTHATCHES

Red-breasted Nuthatch
(Sitta canadensis)

BREEDING RANGE: Labrador west to southern Alaska, south to southern California, east to central New Mexico, north to western Montana; northern Minnesota east to New Jersey; mountains to Georgia

WINTER RANGE: Wanders irregularly to southern Arizona, New Mexico and Texas, the Gulf states and Florida, retreats from more northern part of range

PREFERRED HABITAT: Conifer forests

PREFERRED NEST SITE: Cavity in dead conifer, birdhouse

CLUTCH SIZE: 4 to 7, usually 5 or 8

INCUBATION PERIOD: 12 days

NESTLING PERIOD: 21 days

BROODS PER SEASON: 1

PREFERRED FOOD: Insects, seeds

SITTIDAE—
NUTHATCHES

Brown-headed Nuthatch
(Sitta pusilla)

BREEDING RANGE: Coastal Delaware south to Florida, west to eastern Texas

WINTER RANGE: Permanent resident in breeding range

PREFERRED HABITAT: Pine woods, cypress swamps

PREFERRED NEST SITE: Dead pine, post, utility pole

CLUTCH SIZE: 5 or 6

INCUBATION PERIOD: 14 days

NESTLING PERIOD: Not known

BROODS PER SEASON: 1

PREFERRED FOOD: Insects, pine seeds

3½″ L

4¾″ L

SITTIDAE—
NUTHATCHES

Pygmy Nuthatch
(Sitta pygmaea)

BREEDING RANGE: Southern British Columbia
east to western Montana, south to central Washington and south to Baja California; Black Hills southwest to eastern Nevada, south to Mexico

WINTER RANGE: Permanent resident in breeding
range

PREFERRED HABITAT: Pine forests

PREFERRED NEST SITE: Cavity in conifer

CLUTCH SIZE: 4 to 9

INCUBATION PERIOD: About 14 days

NESTLING PERIOD: Not known

BROODS PER YEAR: 1

PREFERRED FOOD: Insects

CERTHIIDAE—
CREEPERS

Brown Creeper
(Certhia americana)

BREEDING RANGE: Newfoundland west to Alaska,
south to mountains of southern California to Mexico
north to southern Alberta, east to New Jersey, mountains to Georgia

WINTER RANGE: Pennsylvania northwest to southern Alberta south to northern Mexico east to Florida;
southwest California

PREFERRED HABITAT: Woodlands, swamps,
shade trees

PREFERRED NEST SITE: Under strip of bark low
on tree

CLUTCH SIZE: 4 to 9, usually 5 or 6

INCUBATION PERIOD: 11 to 15 days

NESTLING PERIOD: 13 to 15 days

BROODS PER SEASON: 1 or 2

PREFERRED FOOD: Insects, insect and spider
eggs and larvae

4 ¼ " L

3 ¼ " L

TROGLODYTIDAE—
WRENS

House Wren
(Troglodytes aedon)

BREEDING RANGE: New Brunswick west to British Columbia, south to southern California, east to north Texas, Missouri, and south Carolina

WINTER RANGE: South Carolina west to California and south to southern Mexico

PREFERRED HABITAT: Woods, thickets, farms, gardens

PREFERRED NEST SITE: Any cavity, including birdhouse

CLUTCH SIZE: 5 to 8, usually 6 or 7

INCUBATION PERIOD: 12 to 15 days

NESTLING PERIOD: 12 to 18 days

BROODS PER SEASON: 2

PREFERRED FOOD: Insects

TROGLODYTIDAE—
WRENS

Winter Wren
(Troglodytes troglodytes)

BREEDING RANGE: Newfoundland west to southern Alaska, south through British Columbia to central California; Washington, northern Idaho, along coast; Appalachians south to northern Georgia

WINTER RANGE: Southern New England west to southern Illinois southwest to the Gulf states; Alaska south to southern California, east through central Arizona, southern New Mexico to Texas

PREFERRED HABITAT: Coniferous forests to brush piles

PREFERRED NEST SITE: Tangle near ground

CLUTCH SIZE: 4 to 7, usually 5 or 6

INCUBATION PERIOD: 14 to 16 days

NESTLING PERIOD: 14 days

BROODS PER SEASON: 2

PREFERRED FOOD: Insects

4½″ L

4¾″ L

TROGLODYTIDAE—
WRENS

Bewick's Wren
(Thryomanes bewickii)

BREEDING RANGE: Southwestern British Columbia southeast to Utah and southwestern Colorado,
east to central Pennsylvania, south to Arkansas, west
to central Texas and central Mexico, west to California and Baja California

WINTER RANGE: Permanent resident throughout
most of its breeding range; south to Gulf states

PREFERRED HABITAT: Woodlands, thickets,
farms, gardens

PREFERRED NEST SITE: Cavity or birdhouse

CLUTCH SIZE: 4 to 11, usually 5 to 7

INCUBATION PERIOD: 14 days

NESTLING PERIOD: 14 days

BROODS PER SEASON: 2, 3 in the South

PREFERRED FOOD: Insects

TROGLODYTIDAE—
WRENS

Carolina Wren
(Thryothorus ludovicianus)

BREEDING RANGE: Southern New England and
central New York west to Iowa, south to Gulf coast
and Mexico

WINTER RANGE: Permanent resident in breeding
range

PREFERRED HABITAT: Thickets, gardens

PREFERRED NEST SITE: Any cavity or birdhouse

CLUTCH SIZE: 4 to 8, usually 5

INCUBATION PERIOD: 12 to 14 days

NESTLING PERIOD: 12 to 14 days

BROODS PER SEASON: 2 or 3

PREFERRED FOOD: Insects

9" L

7¾" L

MIMIDAE—
MOCKINGBIRDS AND THRASHERS

Northern Mockingbird
(Mimus polyglottos)

BREEDING RANGE: Southeastern Maine west to northern California, south Mexico to the Gulf states and Florida

WINTER RANGE: Permanent resident in most of breeding range; partially migratory in northernmost parts, retreating southward

PREFERRED HABITAT: Deserts and brush to farms to cities

PREFERRED NEST SITE: Bush or dense tree

CLUTCH SIZE: 3 to 6, usually 4 or 5

INCUBATION PERIOD: 12 to 14 days

NESTLING PERIOD: 10 to 13 days

BROODS PER SEASON: 2, often 3 in the South

PREFERRED FOOD: Insects, fruits, berries, seeds

MIMIDAE—
MOCKINGBIRDS AND THRASHERS

Catbird
(Dumetella carolinensis)

BREEDING RANGE: Nova Scotia west to British Columbia, south to eastern Oregon and northern Utah to east Texas and south to Gulf states except Florida

WINTER RANGE: Coastal areas from Long Island south to Florida and the Gulf states and Mexico

PREFERRED HABITAT: Wet or dry thickets, hedges

PREFERRED NEST SITE: Near ground in thicket

CLUTCH SIZE: 3 to 6, usually 4

INCUBATION PERIOD: 12 to 15 days

NESTLING PERIOD: 9 to 16 days, usually 10 or 11

BROODS PER SEASON: 2, sometimes 3

PREFERRED FOOD: Insects, fruits, berries

MIMIDAE—
MOCKINGBIRDS AND THRASHERS

Brown Thrasher
(Toxostoma rufum)

BREEDING RANGE: Maine west to southern Alberta, south to the Gulf states and Florida

WINTER RANGE: Long Island and coastal New Jersey to coastal Virginia, inland from Virginia west to Texas, south to the Gulf states and Florida

PREFERRED HABITAT: Dry thickets

PREFERRED NEST SITE: Thicket

CLUTCH SIZE: 2 to 6, usually 4

INCUBATION PERIOD: 11 to 14 days

NESTLING PERIOD: 12 to 13 days

BROODS PER SEASON: 2, sometimes 3 in the South

PREFERRED FOOD: Insects, berries, fruits, grains

MIMIDAE—
MOCKINGBIRDS AND THRASHERS

California Thrasher
(Toxostoma redivivum)

BREEDING RANGE: Sacramento Valley in California to northern Baja California

WINTER RANGE: Permanent resident in breeding range

PREFERRED HABITAT: Chaparral, thickets, parks, gardens

PREFERRED NEST SITE: Bush

CLUTCH SIZE: 2 to 4

INCUBATION PERIOD: 14 days

NESTLING PERIOD: 12 to 14 days

BROODS PER SEASON: 2

PREFERRED FOOD: Wild fruits, berries, insects

7" L

8½" L

MIMIDAE—
MOCKINGBIRDS AND THRASHERS

Sage Thrasher
(Oreoscoptes montanus)

BREEDING RANGE: Southern British Columbia, central Montana, and Idaho to southern California and Nevada, northern Arizona and northern New Mexico; an isolated community in southwestern Saskatchewan

WINTER RANGE: Central California east to central Texas, south to Mexico

PREFERRED HABITAT: Brush, deserts

PREFERRED NEST SITE: Bush

CLUTCH SIZE: 4 to 7, usually 4 or 5

INCUBATION PERIOD: Averages 15 days

NESTLING PERIOD: Not known

BROODS PER SEASON: 1, sometimes 2

PREFERRED FOOD: Insects, berries, fruits

MUSCICAPIDAE—
THRUSHES, KINGLETS, AND GNATCATCHERS

Robin
(Turdus migratorius)

BREEDING RANGE: Labrador west to Alaska, south to Mexico, east to Florida

WINTER RANGE: Southern New Brunswick west to British Columbia, south to Mexico, the Gulf coast, and Florida

PREFERRED HABITAT: Open woods and swamps to cities

PREFERRED NEST SITE: Tree or nesting box

CLUTCH SIZE: 2 to 7, usually 3 or 4

INCUBATION PERIOD: 11 to 14 days

NESTLING PERIOD: 9 to 16 days

BROODS PER SEASON: 2 or 3

PREFERRED FOOD: Fruits, earthworms, insects

7" L

6" L

MUSCICAPIDAE—
THRUSHES, KINGLETS, AND GNATCATCHERS

Wood Thrush
(Hylocichla mustelina)

BREEDING RANGE: Nova Scotia to South Dakota, south to Texas and east to Florida

WINTER RANGE: Coastal Mexico and Central America

PREFERRED HABITAT: Moist woods, shade trees

PREFERRED NEST SITE: Tree or shrub

CLUTCH SIZE: 2 to 5, usually 3 or 4

INCUBATION PERIOD: 13 to 14 days

NESTLING PERIOD: 12 to 14 days

BROODS PER SEASON: 1 or 2, 3 in the South

PREFERRED FOOD: Insects, fruits

MUSCICAPIDAE—
THRUSHES, KINGLETS, AND GNATCATCHERS

Hermit Thrush
(Catharus guttatus)

BREEDING RANGE: Labrador west to Alaska, south to high mountains of California and the Rockies; central Minnesota to southern New York, mountains of West Virginia and Maryland

WINTER RANGE: New Jersey and southern Ohio south to Gulf states and Florida; southwest British Columbia, California to Texas and south to Mexico and Central America

PREFERRED HABITAT: Damp mixed woods, thickets

PREFERRED NEST SITE: On ground or in small tree

CLUTCH SIZE: 3 to 6, usually 3 or 4

INCUBATION PERIOD: 12 days

NESTLING PERIOD: 12 days

BROODS PER SEASON: 1 to 3

PREFERRED FOOD: Insects, fruits

6¼" L

6" L

MUSCICAPIDAE—
THRUSHES, KINGLETS, AND GNATCATCHERS

Swainson's Thrush
(Catharus ustulatus) (Olive-backed Thrush)

BREEDING RANGE: Labrador west to Alaska; in East, south to Virginia; in West, south to southern California and the mountains of the West to northern New Mexico

WINTER RANGE: Central and South America

PREFERRED HABITAT: Thickets, river woods, conifers

PREFERRED NEST SITE: Bush or small tree

CLUTCH SIZE: 3 to 5, usually 4

INCUBATION PERIOD: 10 to 13 days

NESTLING PERIOD: 10 to 12 days

BROODS PER SEASON: 1

PREFERRED FOOD: Insects, wild fruits

MUSCICAPIDAE—
THRUSHES, KINGLETS, AND GNATCATCHERS

Veery
(Catharus fuscescens)

BREEDING RANGE: In East, Newfoundland south to northern Georgia; west to British Columbia south through northern Great Basin and the Rockies to northern Nevada, southern Colorado; east central Arizona

WINTER RANGE: South America

PREFERRED HABITAT: Damp woods with thick undergrowth

PREFERRED NEST SITE: On or near ground in undergrowth

CLUTCH SIZE: 3 to 5, usually 4

INCUBATION PERIOD: 10 to 12 days

NESTLING PERIOD: 16 days

BROODS PER SEASON: 1 or 2

PREFERRED FOOD: Insects, wild fruits, seeds

MUSCICAPIDAE—
THRUSHES, KINGLETS, AND GNATCATCHERS

Eastern Bluebird
(Sialia sialis)

BREEDING RANGE: Nova Scotia west to south-eastern Saskatchewan, south through Texas to Central America, east along the Gulf states to Florida; southeastern Arizona

WINTER RANGE: Southern New England west to eastern New Mexico and south to Mexico

PREFERRED HABITAT: Orchards, wood edges, farms

PREFERRED NEST SITE: Cavities in trees, bird-houses

CLUTCH SIZE: 3 to 7, usually 4 or 5

INCUBATION PERIOD: 13 to 15 days

NESTLING PERIOD: 15 to 20 days

BROODS PER SEASON: 2 or 3

PREFERRED FOOD: Insects, fruits

MUSCICAPIDAE—
THRUSHES, KINGLETS, AND GNATCATCHERS

Western Bluebird
(Sialia mexicana)

BREEDING RANGE: Southern British Columbia and western Montana south to west Texas and central Mexico and west to southern California

WINTER RANGE: Puget Sound, southern Utah, and southwestern Colorado south

PREFERRED HABITAT: Open woods, farms, deserts

PREFERRED NEST SITE: Cavity in tree, bird-house

CLUTCH SIZE: 4 to 8, usually 4 to 6

INCUBATION PERIOD: 13 to 15 days

NESTLING PERIOD: 14 to 18 days

BROODS PER SEASON: 2

PREFERRED FOOD: Insects, fruits, berries, weed seeds

6" L

6¾" L

MUSCICAPIDAE—
THRUSHES, KINGLETS, AND GNATCATCHERS

Mountain Bluebird
(Sialia currucoides)

BREEDING RANGE: Southern Yukon east to
southwestern Manitoba, south through northeastern
North Dakota and the Black Hills to central New
Mexico and west through high mountains to southern California

WINTER RANGE: Washington to Colorado south
to northern Mexico

PREFERRED HABITAT: Open terrain

PREFERRED NEST SITE: Cavity in tree or cliff,
birdhouse

CLUTCH SIZE: 4 to 8, usually 4 to 6

INCUBATION PERIOD: 14 days

NESTLING PERIOD: 12 to 14 days

BROODS PER SEASON: 2

PREFERRED FOOD: Insects, fruits

MUSCICAPIDAE—
THRUSHES, KINGLETS, AND GNATCATCHERS

Townsend's Solitaire
(Myadestes townsendi)

BREEDING RANGE: Central and eastern Alaska
to southwestern Mackenzie, south to central New
Mexico and west through the mountains to southern California

WINTER RANGE: Southern British Columbia and
Alberta south to northern Mexico and central Texas

PREFERRED HABITAT: Mountain forests, can-
yons

PREFERRED NEST SITE: On the ground

CLUTCH SIZE: 3 to 5, usually 4

INCUBATION PERIOD: Not known

NESTLING PERIOD: Not known

BROODS PER SEASON: 1, perhaps 2

PREFERRED FOOD: Flying insects

4″ L

3¾″ L

MUSCICAPIDAE—
THRUSHES, KINGLETS, AND GNATCATCHERS

Blue-gray Gnatcatcher
(Polioptila caerulea)

BREEDING RANGE: Central New England, central Minnesota west to northeastern California, south to southern Mexico and Florida

WINTER RANGE: North Carolina south along coast to Florida and Gulf coastal areas, west to southern California and south to Central America

PREFERRED HABITAT: Open mixed woods, thickets, gardens with tall trees

PREFERRED NEST SITE: Horizontal limb on tall tree

CLUTCH SIZE: 3 to 5, usually 4 or 5

INCUBATION PERIOD: 13 to 15 days

NESTLING PERIOD: 10 to 13 days

BROODS PER SEASON: 1 or 2

PREFERRED FOOD: Insects

MUSCICAPIDAE—
THRUSHES, KINGLETS, AND GNATCATCHERS

Golden-crowned Kinglet
(Regulus satrapa)

BREEDING RANGE: In the East, Newfoundland west to Manitoba, south to Wisconsin, south in mountains to North Carolina. In the West, southern Alaska south to California, east to New Mexico; north central Mexico

WINTER RANGE: Retreats from northernmost part of breeding range except southern Alaska

PREFERRED HABITAT: Conifers, mixed or deciduous woods, thickets

PREFERRED NEST SITE: Horizontal branch of conifer

CLUTCH SIZE: 5 to 11, usually 8 or 9

INCUBATION PERIOD: Probably 14 to 15 days

NESTLING PERIOD: Not known

BROODS PER SEASON: 2

PREFERRED FOOD: Insects

3¾" L

7" L

MUSCICAPIDAE—
THRUSHES, KINGLETS, AND GNATCATCHERS

Ruby-crowned Kinglet
(Regulus calendula)

BREEDING RANGE: Labrador west to Alaska, south to east central California, east to New Mexico; absent from central portion of country, east in Canada from northern Great Lakes to northern Maine

WINTER RANGE: Southern New England south and west to Florida, Texas; northern California south to Central America; southeast Oregon, central Nevada

PREFERRED HABITAT: Conifers, shrubbery, orchards

PREFERRED NEST SITE: Coniferous shrub or tree

CLUTCH SIZE: 5 to 11, usually 7 to 9

INCUBATION PERIOD: 12 days

NESTLING PERIOD: 12 days

BROODS PER SEASON: 1

PREFERRED FOOD: Insects, seeds, fruits

BOMBYCILLIDAE—
WAXWINGS

Cedar Waxwing
(Bombycilla cedrorum)

BREEDING RANGE: Newfoundland west to central British Columbia south to central California, east to Oklahoma, northern Georgia

WINTER RANGE: Southern Nova Scotia west to eastern Nevada, southern California south to Central America; southern British Columbia to central California

PREFERRED HABITAT: Open woods, edges, orchards

PREFERRED NEST SITE: Horizontal branch on tree; semicolonial

CLUTCH SIZE: 2 to 6, usually 4 or 5

INCUBATION PERIOD: 12 to 16 days

NESTLING PERIOD: 12 to 18 days

BROODS PER SEASON: 1 or 2

PREFERRED FOOD: Berries, insects

9″ L

6″ L

LANIIDAE—
SHRIKES

Loggerhead Shrike
(Lanius ludovicianus)

BREEDING RANGE: Virginia west to northern Alberta, south to southern Mexico and Florida

WINTER RANGE: Virginia west to Oregon and south to southern Mexico and Florida

PREFERRED HABITAT: Scattered trees in open country, deserts, and farms

PREFERRED NEST SITE: Bush or tree

CLUTCH SIZE: 4 to 8, usually 4 to 6

INCUBATION PERIOD: 16 days

NESTLING PERIOD: 16 to 20 days

BROODS PER SEASON: 1 or 2

PREFERRED FOOD: Insects, small animals, and birds

STURNIDAE—
STARLINGS

Starling
(Sturnus vulgaris)

BREEDING RANGE: Southern Canada, throughout United States except southernmost Texas to northern Mexico

WINTER RANGE: Resident within breeding range

PREFERRED HABITAT: Farmlands to cities

PREFERRED NEST SITE: Cavity in tree, birdhouse

CLUTCH SIZE: 2 to 8, usually 4 to 6

INCUBATION PERIOD: 11 to 13 days

NESTLING PERIOD: 16 to 22 days

BROODS PER SEASON: 2 to 3

PREFERRED FOOD: Insects, seeds, fruits, grains

6" L

5" L

VIREONIDAE—
VIREOS

White-eyed Vireo
(Vireo griseus)

BREEDING RANGE: Southern New England west to Nebraska, Texas south to Mexico, the Gulf states, and Florida

WINTER RANGE: South Georgia coast south to Florida, Gulf coast, and south to Mexico

PREFERRED HABITAT: Thickets

PREFERRED NEST SITE: Low branch of sapling or shrub with surrounding vegetation

CLUTCH SIZE: 3 to 5, usually 4

INCUBATION PERIOD: 14 to 15 days

NESTLING PERIOD: Not known

BROODS PER SEASON: 1

PREFERRED FOOD: Insects, wild fruits

VIREONIDAE—
VIREOS

Yellow-throated Vireo
(Vireo flavifrons)

BREEDING RANGE: Maine west to Saskatchewan, south to Texas, Gulf states, and Florida

WINTER RANGE: South Florida; southwestern Louisiana to South America along coast

PREFERRED HABITAT: Shade trees, orchards

PREFERRED NEST SITE: Deciduous trees

CLUTCH SIZE: 3 to 5, usually 3 or 4

INCUBATION PERIOD: 14 days

NESTLING PERIOD: 14 days

BROODS PER SEASON: 1

PREFERRED FOOD: Insects

5″ L

4¾″ L

VIREONIDAE—
VIREOS

Red-eyed Vireo
(Vireo olivaceus)

BREEDING RANGE: Nova Scotia west to North-west Territories and British Columbia, southeast to Texas, Gulf states, and Florida

WINTER RANGE: South America

PREFERRED HABITAT: Woodlands or shade trees

PREFERRED NEST SITE: Bush, tree

CLUTCH SIZE: 2 to 5

INCUBATION PERIOD: 12 to 14 days

NESTLING PERIOD: 10 to 12 days

BROODS PER SEASON: 1 or 2

PREFERRED FOOD: Insects

VIREONIDAE—
VIREOS

Warbling Vireo
(Vireo gilvus)

BREEDING RANGE: Nova Scotia west to North-west Territories and southeast Alaska, south to Baja California, northern Mexico, Louisiana northeast to North Carolina

WINTER RANGE: South America

PREFERRED HABITAT: Woods, shade trees

PREFERRED NEST SITE: Slender branch of tree

CLUTCH SIZE: 3 to 5, usually 4

INCUBATION PERIOD: 12 days

NESTLING PERIOD: 16 days

BROODS PER SEASON: 1

PREFERRED FOOD: Insects

5¼" L

4½" L

PLOCEIDAE—
WEAVER FINCHES

House Sparrow
(Passer domesticus)

BREEDING RANGE: Throughout inhabited United States and Canada

WINTER RANGE: Permanent resident

PREFERRED HABITAT: Farms, villages, cities

PREFERRED NEST SITE: Cavities, crevices in buildings, trees, vines, birdhouses

CLUTCH SIZE: 3 to 7, usually 5

INCUBATION PERIOD: 12 to 13 days

NESTLING PERIOD: 13 to 18 days

BROODS PER SEASON: 2, sometimes 3 or 4

PREFERRED FOOD: Insects, seeds, garbage

EMBERIZIDAE—
WOOD WARBLERS, SPARROWS, BLACK-BIRDS, AND TANAGERS

Black-and-white Warbler
(Mniotilta varia)

BREEDING RANGE: Southern Canada through southwestern Northwest Territories to northeastern British Columbia, south through eastern Montana to central Texas and Louisiana northeast to South Carolina

WINTER RANGE: Florida, southern Texas, Gulf states coastally south through the tropics to South America; Baja California south

PREFERRED HABITAT: Woodlands

PREFERRED NEST SITE: Stump, on ground

CLUTCH SIZE: 4 to 5

INCUBATION PERIOD: 13 days

NESTLING PERIOD: 11 to 12 days

BROODS PER SEASON: 1

PREFERRED FOOD: Insects

4½-5½" L

4¼" L

EMBERIZIDAE—
WOOD WARBLERS, SPARROWS, BLACK-
BIRDS, AND TANAGERS

Orange-crowned Warbler
(Vermivora celata)

BREEDING RANGE: North central Alaska across
Canada to just north of the Great Lakes, western
Montana south to west Texas, west to Baja California

WINTER RANGE: Southern United States to Guat-
emala

PREFERRED HABITAT: Open woodlands, brush

PREFERRED NEST SITE: On ground or in low
shrub

CLUTCH SIZE: 4 to 6, usually 4 or 5

INCUBATION PERIOD: 12 to 14 days

NESTLING PERIOD: 8 to 10 days

BROODS PER SEASON: Not known

PREFERRED FOOD: Insects

EMBERIZIDAE—
WOOD WARBLERS, SPARROWS, BLACK-
BIRDS, AND TANAGERS

Yellow Warbler
(Dendroica petechia)

BREEDING RANGE: Canada and Alaska south to
northern South America except Texas, Louisiana,
southern Gulf states; Florida Keys

WINTER RANGE: Southern California, southwest
Arizona south to Central and South America

PREFERRED HABITAT: Willows, farmlands,
dense shrubbery, gardens

PREFERRED NEST SITE: Shrub, tree

CLUTCH SIZE: 3 to 5, usually 4 or 5

INCUBATION PERIOD: 10 to 11 days

NESTLING PERIOD: 9 to 12 days

BROODS PER SEASON: 1

PREFERRED FOOD: Insects

4 ¼ " L

4 ¾ " L

EMBERIZIDAE—
WOOD WARBLERS, SPARROWS, BLACK-
BIRDS, AND TANAGERS

Magnolia Warbler
(Dendroica magnolia)

BREEDING RANGE: Newfoundland through
Northwest Territories, south through eastern British
Columbia to Great Lakes area to Massachusetts and
south to mountains of North Carolina

WINTER RANGE: Mexico south to Panama

PREFERRED HABITAT: Coniferous forests,
edges, gardens

PREFERRED NEST SITE: Horizontal branch of
small conifer

CLUTCH SIZE: 3 to 6, usually 4 or 5

INCUBATION PERIOD: 12 days

NESTLING PERIOD: 10 days

BROODS PER SEASON: 2

PREFERRED FOOD: Insects

EMBERIZIDAE—
WOOD WARBLERS, SPARROWS, BLACK-
BIRDS, AND TANAGERS

Yellow-rumped Warbler
(Dendroica coronata)

BREEDING RANGE: Alaska and Canada south to
mountains of Massachusetts, New York, and Pennsylvania

WINTER RANGE: Southern New England southwest to central California and south to Central America; along Pacific coast from southwestern British
Columbia south

PREFERRED HABITAT: Forests to gardens

PREFERRED NEST SITE: Conifer

CLUTCH SIZE: 3 to 5, usually 4 or 5

INCUBATION PERIOD: 12 to 13 days

NESTLING PERIOD: 12 to 14 days

BROODS PER SEASON: 1 or 2

PREFERRED FOOD: Insects, berries

4½″ L

4¼″ L

EMBERIZIDAE—
WOOD WARBLERS, SPARROWS, BLACK-
BIRDS, AND TANAGERS

Yellow-throated Warbler
(Dendroica dominica)

BREEDING RANGE: Southern New Jersey west to
Missouri, eastern Oklahoma and Texas, Louisiana
to Florida

WINTER RANGE: Southern Georgia and Florida
to the tropics

PREFERRED HABITAT: Bottomlands

PREFERRED NEST SITE: Branch of pine, oak,
sycamore

CLUTCH SIZE: 4

INCUBATION PERIOD: Probably 12 to 13 days

NESTLING PERIOD: Not known

BROODS PER SEASON: 1, 2 in the South

PREFERRED FOOD: Insects

EMBERIZIDAE—
WOOD WARBLERS, SPARROWS, BLACK-
BIRDS, AND TANAGERS

Palm Warbler
(Dendroica palmarum)

BREEDING RANGE: Southern Labrador west to
Northwest Territories, Alberta, south to northern
Minnesota, southern Ontario to Nova Scotia

WINTER RANGE: Virginia southwest to Florida,
Texas, and Mexico

PREFERRED HABITAT: Bogs, lawns

PREFERRED NEST SITE: Ground at foot of bush
or tree; sometimes in loose colonies

CLUTCH SIZE: 4 or 5

INCUBATION PERIOD: 12 days

NESTLING PERIOD: 12 days

BROODS PER SEASON: 1 or 2

PREFERRED FOOD: Insects, berries

4¼ " L

6¼ " L

EMBERIZIDAE—
WOOD WARBLERS, SPARROWS, BLACK-
BIRDS, AND TANAGERS

Common Yellowthroat
(Geothlypis trichas)

BREEDING RANGE: Central Canada south to
southern Mexico

WINTER RANGE: Southern Maryland south to
Texas, west to California, south to Central America

PREFERRED HABITAT: Swamps, thickets

PREFERRED NEST SITE: Weeds, shrubs

CLUTCH SIZE: 3 to 6, usually 4

INCUBATION PERIOD: 11 to 13 days

NESTLING PERIOD: 9 to 10 days

BROODS PER SEASON: 1 or 2

PREFERRED FOOD: Insects

EMBERIZIDAE
WOOD WARBLERS, SPARROWS, BLACK-
BIRDS, AND TANAGERS

Yellow-breasted Chat
(Icteria virens)

BREEDING RANGE: New Hampshire west to
southern British Columbia, south to northern Baja
California, northern Mexico, Texas to northern Florida

WINTER RANGE: Mexico and Central America to
Panama

PREFERRED HABITAT: Thickets, briars, brushy
pastures

PREFERRED NEST SITE: Thicket

CLUTCH SIZE: 3 to 5, usually 4

INCUBATION PERIOD: 8 days

NESTLING PERIOD: Not known

BROODS PER SEASON: 1

PREFERRED FOOD: Insects, berries

EMBERIZIDAE—
WOOD WARBLERS, SPARROWS, BLACK-
BIRDS, AND TANAGERS

American Redstart
(Setophaga ruticilla)

BREEDING RANGE: Southern Labrador west to
Northwest Territories, southeast Alaska south to
Oregon, southeast to eastern Texas and Louisiana to
mountains of Georgia

WINTER RANGE: Mexico to Ecuador, south Florida

PREFERRED HABITAT: Deciduous woodlands,
swamps, shrubbery, shade trees

PREFERRED NEST SITE: Bush or tree

CLUTCH SIZE: 3 to 5, usually 4

INCUBATION PERIOD: 12 to 14 days

NESTLING PERIOD: 8 to 9 days

BROODS PER SEASON: 1

PREFERRED FOOD: Insects

EMBERIZIDAE—
WOOD WARBLERS, SPARROWS, BLACK-
BIRDS, AND TANAGERS

Bobolink
(Dolichonyx oryzivorus)

BREEDING RANGE: Nova Scotia west to southern British Columbia, south through eastern Washington to Colorado, east to coastal Maryland

WINTER RANGE: South America

PREFERRED HABITAT: Open grasslands

PREFERRED NEST SITE: On ground in dense
vegetation

CLUTCH SIZE: 4 to 7, usually 5 or 6

INCUBATION PERIOD: 13 days

NESTLING PERIOD: 10 to 14 days

BROODS PER SEASON: 1

PREFERRED FOOD: Insects, seeds

9″ L

8½″ L

EMBERIZIDAE—
WOOD WARBLERS, SPARROWS, BLACK-
BIRDS, AND TANAGERS

Eastern Meadowlark
(Sturnella magna)

BREEDING RANGE: New Brunswick west to
Ontario, south through Nebraska to Texas and eastern Arizona to northern Mexico, east to Florida

WINTER RANGE: Central New England to Great
Lakes and south

PREFERRED HABITAT: Meadows

PREFERRED NEST SITE: On ground in vegetation

CLUTCH SIZE: 2 to 6, usually 3 to 5

INCUBATION PERIOD: 13 to 15 days

NESTLING PERIOD: 10 to 12 days

BROODS PER SEASON: 2

PREFERRED FOOD: Insects, seeds, grains

EMBERIZIDAE
WOOD WARBLERS, SPARROWS, BLACK-
BIRDS, AND TANAGERS

Western Meadowlark
(Sturnella neglecta)

BREEDING RANGE: Central British Columbia to
southern Ontario, south to northeastern Louisiana,
west through Texas and northern Mexico to Baja California

WINTER RANGE: Southwest British Columbia
south and east to Gulf states, south to central Mexico

PREFERRED HABITAT: Meadows, fields, prairies

PREFERRED NEST SITE: On ground in grass

CLUTCH SIZE: 3 to 7

INCUBATION PERIOD: 13 to 15 days

NESTLING PERIOD: About 12 days

BROODS PER SEASON: 2

PREFERRED FOOD: Insects, grains

8½" L

7¼" L

EMBERIZIDAE—
WOOD WARBLERS, SPARROWS, BLACK-
BIRDS, AND TANAGERS

Yellow-headed Blackbird
(Xanthocephalus xanthocephalus)

BREEDING RANGE: Central British Columbia east
to southern Manitoba, northwest Ohio southwest to
New Mexico and northern Baja California

WINTER RANGE: Southwestern United States and
Mexico

PREFERRED HABITAT: Fields, marshes, farms

PREFERRED NEST SITE: Attached to cattails in
marshes; in loose colony

CLUTCH SIZE: 3 to 5, usually 4

INCUBATION PERIOD: 12 to 13 days

NESTLING PERIOD: 12 days

BROODS PER SEASON: 1

PREFERRED FOOD: Insects, grains, seeds

EMBERIZIDAE—
WOOD WARBLERS, SPARROWS, BLACK-
BIRDS, AND TANAGERS

Red-winged Blackbird
(Agelaius phoeniceus)

BREEDING RANGE: Newfoundland west to Alaska,
south to Mexico and east to Florida

WINTER RANGE: Southern New England west to
British Columbia, south to South America

PREFERRED HABITAT: Fields, marshes, woods
edges

PREFERRED NEST SITE: Attached to reeds in
marsh; loose colonies

CLUTCH SIZE: 3 to 5, usually 3 or 4

INCUBATION PERIOD: 10 to 12 days

NESTLING PERIOD: 10 to 11 days

BROODS PER SEASON: 2 or 3

PREFERRED FOOD: Insects, seeds, grains

6″ L

6½″ L

EMBERIZIDAE—
WOOD WARBLERS, SPARROWS, BLACK-
BIRDS, AND TANAGERS

Orchard Oriole
(Icterus spurius)

BREEDING RANGE: Eastern Massachusetts west to south central Saskatchewan, south to northern Mexico, the Gulf states, and northern Florida

WINTER RANGE: Mexico to northern South America

PREFERRED HABITAT: Orchards, farmlands, towns

PREFERRED NEST SITE: Branch in dense foliage

CLUTCH SIZE: 3 to 7, usually 4 or 5

INCUBATION PERIOD: 12 to 14 days

NESTLING PERIOD: 11 to 14 days

BROODS PER SEASON: 1

PREFERRED FOOD: Insects, fruits

EMBERIZIDAE—
WOOD WARBLERS, SPARROWS, BLACK-
BIRDS, AND TANAGERS

Northern (Baltimore) Oriole
(Icterus galbula)

BREEDING RANGE: Nova Scotia west to British Columbia, south to southern California and Mexico, east to North Carolina

WINTER RANGE: Mexico to northern South America

PREFERRED HABITAT: Shade trees and woods edges

PREFERRED NEST SITE: High branch of decid-uous tree

CLUTCH SIZE: 3 to 6, usually 4 or 5

INCUBATION PERIOD: 12 to 14 days

NESTLING PERIOD: 11 to 14 days

BROODS PER SEASON: 1

PREFERRED FOOD: Insects, fruits

7″ L

8″ L

EMBERIZIDAE—
WOOD WARBLERS, SPARROWS, BLACK-
BIRDS, AND TANAGERS

Scott's Oriole
(Icterus parisorum)

BREEDING RANGE: Southwestern United States,
northern Mexico

WINTER RANGE: Mexico

PREFERRED HABITAT: Dry woods and scrub

PREFERRED NEST SITE: Yucca, small tree

CLUTCH SIZE: 2 to 4

INCUBATION PERIOD: 14 days

NESTLING PERIOD: 14 days

BROODS PER SEASON: 2

PREFERRED FOOD: Nectar, insects, fruits

EMBERIZIDAE—
WOOD WARBLERS, SPARROWS, BLACK-
BIRDS, AND TANAGERS

Brewer's Blackbird
(Euphagus cyanocephalus)

BREEDING RANGE: Central British Columbia east
to southwestern Ontario, south through Michigan to
New Mexico and west to southern California

WINTER RANGE: Southern British Columbia,
southeast through South Carolina, Florida, and
Mexico

PREFERRED HABITAT: Fields, ranches, farms

PREFERRED NEST SITE: On ground, bush, tree;
loose colonies

CLUTCH SIZE: 4 to 8, usually 4 to 6

INCUBATION PERIOD: 12 to 14 days

NESTLING PERIOD: 13 days

BROODS PER SEASON: 1

PREFERRED FOOD: Insects, seeds

10-12 " L

6½ " L

EMBERIZIDAE—
WOOD WARBLERS, SPARROWS, BLACK-
BIRDS, AND TANAGERS

Common Grackle
(Quiscalus quiscula)

BREEDING RANGE: Newfoundland west to southern Mackenzie, south to New Mexico, the Gulf
states, and Florida

WINTER RANGE: Central New England and New
Jersey west to Kansas, south to eastern Texas, the
Gulf states, and Florida

PREFERRED HABITAT: Croplands, lawns

PREFERRED NEST SITE: Tree, bush; often in
colonies

CLUTCH SIZE: 4 to 6, usually 5

INCUBATION PERIOD: 11 to 13 days

NESTLING PERIOD: 14 to 20 days

BROODS PER SEASON: 1

PREFERRED FOOD: Insects, fruits, grains

EMBERIZIDAE—
WOOD WARBLERS, SPARROWS, BLACK-
BIRDS, AND TANAGERS

Brown-headed Cowbird
(Molothrus ater)

BREEDING RANGE: Newfoundland west to British Columbia, south to Mexico and Louisiana, and
northern Florida

WINTER RANGE: Central New England west to
California, south to Mexico, and east to Florida

PREFERRED HABITAT: Fields, woods edges,
farms

PREFERRED NEST SITE: Parasitic

CLUTCH SIZE: 1 to 6, usually 3

INCUBATION PERIOD: 10 days

NESTLING PERIOD: 10 days

BROODS PER SEASON: 3 or 4

PREFERRED FOOD: Insects, seeds, berries, grains

6¼ " L

6¼ " L

EMBERIZIDAE—
WOOD WARBLERS, SPARROWS, BLACK-
BIRDS, AND TANAGERS

Western Tanager
(Piranga ludoviciana)

BREEDING RANGE: Southeast Alaska, south and
east Mackenzie east to the Black Hills, west Texas,
west to Baja California

WINTER RANGE: Mexico to South America

PREFERRED HABITAT: Open pine and fir forests

PREFERRED NEST SITE: Horizontal branch of
conifer, 5 to 30 feet from the ground

CLUTCH SIZE: 3 to 4

INCUBATION PERIOD: 13 days

NESTLING PERIOD: 13 to 15 days

BROODS PER SEASON: 1

PREFERRED FOOD: Insects, fruits, berries

EMBERIZIDAE—
WOOD WARBLERS, SPARROWS, BLACK-
BIRDS, AND TANAGERS

Scarlet Tanager
(Piranga olivacea)

BREEDING RANGE: Nova Scotia west to southern Saskatchewan, south to eastern Oklahoma, and
east to coast of Virginia

WINTER RANGE: South America

PREFERRED HABITAT: Deciduous and mixed
woodlands

PREFERRED NEST SITE: On an oak branch away
from the trunk, 8 to 75 feet from the ground

CLUTCH SIZE: 3 to 5, usually 4

INCUBATION PERIOD: 13 to 14 days

NESTLING PERIOD: 14 to 16 days

BROODS PER SEASON: 1

PREFERRED FOOD: Insects, fruits

6½" L

7¾" L

EMBERIZIDAE—
WOOD WARBLERS, SPARROWS, BLACK-BIRDS, AND TANAGERS

Summer Tanager
(Piranga rubra)

BREEDING RANGE: Delaware west to southern California and northern Mexico east to the Gulf states and Florida

WINTER RANGE: Mexico, Central and South America

PREFERRED HABITAT: Lowlands and foothills

PREFERRED NEST SITE: Woodlands and groves

CLUTCH SIZE: 3 to 4

INCUBATION PERIOD: 11 to 12 days

NESTLING PERIOD: 7 to 10 days

BROODS PER SEASON: 1

PREFERRED FOOD: Insects

EMBERIZIDAE—
WOOD WARBLERS, SPARROWS, BLACK-BIRDS, AND TANAGERS

Northern Cardinal
(Cardinalis cardinalis)

BREEDING RANGE: New Brunswick west to Great Plains, south to Texas, southern New Mexico, and Arizona, Mexico east to Florida

WINTER RANGE: Permanent resident in breeding range

PREFERRED HABITAT: Open woodland, parks, gardens, suburbs

PREFERRED NEST SITE: Shrubs, small trees

CLUTCH SIZE: 2 to 5, usually 3 or 4

INCUBATION PERIOD: 12 to 13 days

NESTLING PERIOD: 9 to 14 days

BROODS PER SEASON: 1 to 3

PREFERRED FOOD: Seeds, fruits, grains, insects

EMBERIZIDAE—
WOOD WARBLERS, SPARROWS, BLACK-
BIRDS, AND TANAGERS

Rose-breasted Grosbeak
(Pheucticus ludovicianus)

BREEDING RANGE: Nova Scotia west to northeastern British Columbia, eastern Colorado south to
Oklahoma and east through Ohio and New Jersey,
mountains to northern Georgia

WINTER RANGE: Mexico to South America

PREFERRED HABITAT: Edges of moist second-
growth woods; suburbs

PREFERRED NEST SITE: Fork of deciduous tree,
from 5 to 25 feet from ground

CLUTCH SIZE: 3 to 6, usually 4

INCUBATION PERIOD: 12 to 14 days

NESTLING PERIOD: 9 to 12 days

BROODS PER SEASON: 1, sometimes 2

PREFERRED FOOD: Insects, seeds, fruits

EMBERIZIDAE—
WOOD WARBLERS, SPARROWS, BLACK-
BIRDS, AND TANAGERS

Black-headed Grosbeak
(Pheucticus melanocephalus)

BREEDING RANGE: Southern British Columbia
east to western North Dakota south to northeast
Kansas south through western United States to southern Mexico

WINTER RANGE: Mexico

PREFERRED HABITAT: Mixed woods, piñons,
orchards, parks

PREFERRED NEST SITE: Tree or bush

CLUTCH SIZE: 3 to 4

INCUBATION PERIOD: Probably 12 days

NESTLING PERIOD: Usually 12 days

BROODS PER SEASON: 1

PREFERRED FOOD: Insects, fruits

6¼" L

5½" L

EMBERIZIDAE—
WOOD WARBLERS, SPARROWS, BLACK-
BIRDS, AND TANAGERS

Blue Grosbeak
(Guiraca caerulea)

BREEDING RANGE: North central California east
to New Jersey, south to Florida, west through north
central Mexico to north central Baja California

WINTER RANGE: South central Arizona through
Mexico to Panama

PREFERRED HABITAT: Brush, thickets, farms

PREFERRED NEST SITE: Bush or low tree

CLUTCH SIZE: 3 to 5

INCUBATION PERIOD: 11 days

NESTLING PERIOD: 13 days

BROODS PER SEASON: 2, at least in the South

PREFERRED FOOD: Insects, grains

EMBERIZIDAE—
WOOD WARBLERS, SPARROWS, BLACK-
BIRDS, AND TANAGERS

Indigo Bunting
(Passerina cyanea)

BREEDING RANGE: Maine west to southern Manitoba, southwest to southeastern California and east
to northern Florida; absent from west Texas, Oklahoma panhandle

WINTER RANGE: Central Mexico south to Panama,
Cuba, Jamaica, and the Bahamas; south Florida

PREFERRED HABITAT: Roadsides, brush, edges
of woods

PREFERRED NEST SITE: Underbrush, thickets

CLUTCH SIZE: 2 to 6, usually 3 or 4

INCUBATION PERIOD: 12 to 13 days

NESTLING PERIOD: 10 to 13 days

BROODS PER SEASON: Often 2

PREFERRED FOOD: Insects, seeds

EMBERIZIDAE—
WOOD WARBLERS, SPARROWS, BLACK-
BIRDS, AND TANAGERS

Lazuli Bunting
(Passerina amoena)

BREEDING RANGE: Great Plains and southern
Saskatchewan west to British Columbia and south to
northwestern Baja California

WINTER RANGE: Southeastern Arizona, Mexico

PREFERRED HABITAT: Dry brushy areas

PREFERRED NEST SITE: Low brush near water

CLUTCH SIZE: 3 to 4

INCUBATION PERIOD: 12 days

NESTLING PERIOD: 10 to 12 days

BROODS PER SEASON: 2

PREFERRED FOOD: Seeds, insects

EMBERIZIDAE—
WOOD WARBLERS, SPARROWS, BLACK-
BIRDS, AND TANAGERS

Painted Bunting
(Passerina ciris)

BREEDING RANGE: Kansas southeast to Florida
panhandle, south along Gulf coast to northeastern
Mexico, central New Mexico; South Carolina to
northeastern Florida

WINTER RANGE: Southern Florida; Mexico to
Panama and Cuba

PREFERRED HABITAT: Thickets, hedgerows,
gardens

PREFERRED NEST SITE: Crotch of bush

CLUTCH SIZE: 3 to 4

INCUBATION PERIOD: 10 to 12 days

NESTLING PERIOD: 12 to 14 days

BROODS PER SEASON: 2 to 4

PREFERRED FOOD: Seeds, insects

6¼" L

6¼" L

EMBERIZIDAE—
WOOD WARBLERS, SPARROWS, BLACK-BIRDS, AND TANAGERS

Dickcissel
(Spiza americana)

BREEDING RANGE: Southern Michigan west to southeastern Saskatchewan and south to Texas, east to south central Pennsylvania

WINTER RANGE: South America

PREFERRED HABITAT: Open spaces, fields, prairies

PREFERRED NEST SITE: On or close to the ground, concealed by plants

CLUTCH SIZE: 3 to 5, usually 4

INCUBATION PERIOD: 10 to 13 days

NESTLING PERIOD: 10 to 12 days

BROODS PER SEASON: 2

PREFERRED FOOD: Seeds, grains, insects

EMBERIZIDAE—
WOOD WARBLERS, SPARROWS, BLACK-BIRDS, AND TANAGERS

Green-tailed Towhee
(Pipilo chlorura)

BREEDING RANGE: Great Plains west, western Montana south to southern California, Arizona, and New Mexico

WINTER RANGE: Southeastern California, Arizona, and New Mexico south to central Mexico

PREFERRED HABITAT: Brushy hillsides

PREFERRED NEST SITE: Underbrush

CLUTCH SIZE: 3 to 4

INCUBATION PERIOD: 12 to 13 days

NESTLING PERIOD: 10 to 12 days

BROODS PER SEASON: 1 to 3

PREFERRED FOOD: Seeds, wild fruits, insects

7¼" L

7" L

EMBERIZIDAE—
WOOD WARBLERS, SPARROWS, BLACK-
BIRDS, AND TANAGERS

Rufous-sided Towhee
(Pipilo erythrophthalmus)

BREEDING RANGE: Southern Maine west to
southern British Columbia, south to Mexico, east to
Florida

WINTER RANGE: New Jersey west to Texas, north
to southern British Columbia, south; retreats from
mountains

PREFERRED HABITAT: Clearings in or edges of
woods, brush, pastures, shrubs

PREFERRED NEST SITE: On ground in brush, low
in shrub

CLUTCH SIZE: 3 to 6, usually 3 or 4

INCUBATION PERIOD: 12 to 13 days

NESTLING PERIOD: 10 to 12 days

BROODS PER SEASON: 1 to 3, usually 2

PREFERRED FOOD: Insects, seeds, fruits, mast

EMBERIZIDAE—
WOOD WARBLERS, SPARROWS, BLACK-
BIRDS, AND TANAGERS

Harris' Sparrow
(Zonotrichia querula)

BREEDING RANGE: Northwest Territories, northern Saskatchewan, Manitoba, northernmost Ontario

WINTER RANGE: Eastern Colorado to southwest
Iowa south to central Texas

PREFERRED HABITAT: Dwarf timber, thickets

PREFERRED NEST SITE: On ground

CLUTCH SIZE: 3 to 5

INCUBATION PERIOD: 12 to 14 days

NESTLING PERIOD: 13 to 15 days

BROODS PER SEASON: 1

PREFERRED FOOD: Seeds

5 ¼ " L

5 ¼ " L

EMBERIZIDAE—
WOOD WARBLERS, SPARROWS, BLACK-
BIRDS, AND TANAGERS

Dark-eyed Junco
(Junco hyemalis)

BREEDING RANGE: Labrador west to Alaska, south to northeastern New Mexico; northern Minnesota to Pennsylvania and south in mountains to northern Georgia

WINTER RANGE: Retreats from northernmost part of breeding range; winters throughout United States, except south Florida

PREFERRED HABITAT: Coniferous and mixed woods

PREFERRED NEST SITE: On ground

CLUTCH SIZE: 3 to 6, usually 4 or 5

INCUBATION PERIOD: 12 to 13 days

NESTLING PERIOD: 9 to 12 days

BROODS PER SEASON: 1 or 2

PREFERRED FOOD: Insects, wild fruits, seeds

EMBERIZIDAE—
WOOD WARBLERS, SPARROWS, BLACK-
BIRDS, AND TANAGERS

American Tree Sparrow
(Spizella arborea)

BREEDING RANGE: Along edge of tundra from Labrador to Alaska

WINTER RANGE: Maritime provinces west to southeastern British Columbia, south to Nevada, northern New Mexico to Virginia

PREFERRED HABITAT: Open country

PREFERRED NEST SITE: Thickets

CLUTCH SIZE: 4 to 5

INCUBATION PERIOD: 11 to 14 days

NESTLING PERIOD: 12 to 14 days

BROODS PER SEASON: 1

PREFERRED FOOD: Seeds

EMBERIZIDAE—
WOOD WARBLERS, SPARROWS, BLACK-
BIRDS, AND TANAGERS

Chipping Sparrow
(Spizella passerina)

BREEDING RANGE: Western Newfoundland west
to Alaska, south to Central America, east to Gulf
states and Georgia

WINTER RANGE: Southern Maryland west to
Texas and southern California and south

PREFERRED HABITAT: Pine woods, edges of
woods, farms, gardens

PREFERRED NEST SITE: Vines, shrubbery, tree

CLUTCH SIZE: 2 to 5, usually 3 or 4

INCUBATION PERIOD: 11 to 14 days

NESTLING PERIOD: 7 to 10 days

BROODS PER SEASON: 1 to 3, usually 2

PREFERRED FOOD: Insects, seeds

EMBERIZIDAE—
WOOD WARBLERS, SPARROWS, BLACK-
BIRDS, AND TANAGERS

Field Sparrow
(Spizella pusilla)

BREEDING RANGE: Central New England to eastern Montana, south to Texas panhandle, south to the
Gulf states and east to the Atlantic; west central Montana

WINTER RANGE: Southern New England west to
southeastern Colorado, south to Texas and Mexico,
east to Florida

PREFERRED HABITAT: Second growth, brush,
pastures

PREFERRED NEST SITE: On ground or in shrubs

CLUTCH SIZE: 2 to 5, usually 3 or 4

INCUBATION PERIOD: 11 to 13 days

NESTLING PERIOD: 7 to 10 days

BROODS PER SEASON: 1 to 3

PREFERRED FOOD: Insects, seeds

EMBERIZIDAE—
WOOD WARBLERS, SPARROWS, BLACK-
BIRDS, AND TANAGERS

White-crowned Sparrow
(Zonotrichia leucophrys)

BREEDING RANGE: Breeds near the limit of trees
in Alaska and Canada, south along the coast and in
the high mountains to southern California, central
Arizona and northern New Mexico

WINTER RANGE: Southwestern British Columbia south to central Mexico; Ohio Valley and southern New Jersey to Louisiana

PREFERRED HABITAT: Brush, thickets; in
winter, open scrub, roadsides, gardens

PREFERRED NEST SITE: On ground or near
ground in a bush

CLUTCH SIZE: 3 to 5; 6 in the Arctic

INCUBATION PERIOD: 12 to 14 days; 15 to 16
days in Alaska

NESTLING PERIOD: 15 to 16 days

BROODS PER SEASON: 1

PREFERRED FOOD: Insects, seeds

EMBERIZIDAE—
WOOD WARBLERS, SPARROWS, BLACK-
BIRDS, AND TANAGERS

White-throated Sparrow
(Zonotrichia albicollis)

BREEDING RANGE: Labrador west to southern
Yukon, south to Wisconsin, Pennsylvania, New England

WINTER RANGE: Ohio Valley and central New
England south to Mexico, the Gulf states, and Florida; coastal California

PREFERRED HABITAT: Woodland undergrowth,
brush

PREFERRED NEST SITE: On ground

CLUTCH SIZE: 3 to 5, usually 4

INCUBATION PERIOD: 11 to 14 days

NESTLING PERIOD: 12 to 14 days

BROODS PER SEASON: Often 2

PREFERRED FOOD: Insects, seeds, wild fruits

6¼" L

6¼" L

EMBERIZIDAE—
WOOD WARBLERS, SPARROWS, BLACK-
BIRDS, AND TANAGERS

Golden-crowned Sparrow
(Zonotrichia atricapilla)

BREEDING RANGE: Central Alaska to southwestern Yukon to mountains of southern British Columbia and western Alberta

WINTER RANGE: Southwestern British Colum-
bia and Pacific states south to northern Baja California

PREFERRED HABITAT: Boreal scrub, spruce

PREFERRED NEST SITE: Under bush

CLUTCH SIZE: 4 to 5

INCUBATION PERIOD: 12 to 14 days

NESTLING PERIOD: 13 to 15 days

BROODS PER SEASON: 1

PREFERRED FOOD: Seeds

EMBERIZIDAE—
WOOD WARBLERS, SPARROWS, BLACK-
BIRDS, AND TANAGERS

Fox Sparrow
(Passerella iliaca)

BREEDING RANGE: Labrador west to Alaska to
the tree limit; south through the high mountains of
California, Nevada, Utah, Colorado

WINTER RANGE: Coastal Massachusetts west to
southern California and north to southwestern British Columbia

PREFERRED HABITAT: Stunted boreal woodlands and undergrowth; in winter, undergrowth,
parks, gardens

PREFERRED NEST SITE: In a bush or on the
ground

CLUTCH SIZE: 3 to 5

INCUBATION PERIOD: 12 to 14 days

NESTLING PERIOD: 11 to 13 days

BROODS PER SEASON: 2

PREFERRED FOOD: Insects, seeds, fruits

5½" L

7¼" L

EMBERIZIDAE—
WOOD WARBLERS, SPARROWS, BLACK-
BIRDS, AND TANAGERS

Song Sparrow
(Melospiza melodia)

BREEDING RANGE: Newfoundland to Aleutians, south to Mexico and east to the mountains of northern Georgia

WINTER RANGE: Central Maine west to Washington, north to Aleutians, south to central Mexico, east to the Gulf states and Florida

PREFERRED HABITAT: Thickets, shrubbery

PREFERRED NEST SITE: On the ground or in a shrub

CLUTCH SIZE: 3 to 6

INCUBATION PERIOD: 12 to 13 days

NESTLING PERIOD: 10 to 14 days

BROODS PER SEASON: 2, sometimes 3

PREFERRED FOOD: Insects, seeds, fruits

FRINGILLIDAE—
FINCHES

Evening Grosbeak
(Coccothraustes vespertina)

BREEDING RANGE: Nova Scotia west along northern Great Lakes to British Columbia, south to California and mountains of western Mexico

WINTER RANGE: Central New England west to southern Alberta, south to eastern New Mexico, east to North Carolina

PREFERRED HABITAT: Coniferous forests

PREFERRED NEST SITE: Conifer

CLUTCH SIZE: 2 to 5, usually 3 or 4

INCUBATION PERIOD: 12 to 14 days

NESTLING PERIOD: 14 to 16 days

BROODS PER SEASON: 1, possibly 2

PREFERRED FOOD: Buds, fruits, seeds, insects

5½" L

5¼" L

FRINGILLIDAE—
FINCHES

Purple Finch
(Carpodacus purpureus)

BREEDING RANGE: Nova Scotia west to southern Yukon, south through Pacific states; in East, to mountains of West Virginia, west to southern Manitoba

WINTER RANGE: Southern Canada west to southern Manitoba, south to Texas and northern Florida

PREFERRED HABITAT: Edges of woods, coniferous forests, shade trees

PREFERRED NEST SITE: Conifer

CLUTCH SIZE: 3 to 6, usually 4 or 5

INCUBATION PERIOD: 13 days

NESTLING PERIOD: 12 to 14 days

BROODS PER SEASON: 1, sometimes 2

PREFERRED FOOD: Seeds, buds, fruits, insects

FRINGILLIDAE—
FINCHES

House Finch
(Carpodacus mexicanus)

BREEDING RANGE: British Columbia south to central Texas and Mexico; introduced: central New England, New York, Michigan south to Tennessee east to Georgia

WINTER RANGE: Permanent resident in breeding range; also winters west Tennessee to Gulf east to northern Florida

PREFERRED HABITAT: Open woods, inhabited areas

PREFERRED NEST SITE: Practically anywhere

CLUTCH SIZE: 2 to 6, usually 4 or 5

INCUBATION PERIOD: 12 to 16 days

NESTLING PERIOD: 12 to 14 days usually; ranges from 11 to 19 days

BROODS PER SEASON: 1 to 3

PREFERRED FOOD: Seeds, fruits, insects

5″ L

4½″ L

FRINGILLIDAE—
FINCHES

Common Redpoll
(Carduelis flammea)

BREEDING RANGE: Arctic; Newfoundland west
to Alaska east to coastal Greenland

WINTER RANGE: Wanders irregularly, south to
Virginia, west through Nebraska, northern Oregon

PREFERRED HABITAT: Tundra, clearings in
woods, swamps, fields

PREFERRED NEST SITE: Low bush or tree

CLUTCH SIZE: 5 to 6

INCUBATION PERIOD: 14 to 15 days

NESTLING PERIOD: 12 to 14 days

BROODS PER SEASON: 1 or 2

PREFERRED FOOD: Seeds

FRINGILLIDAE—
FINCHES

Pine Siskin
(Carduelis pinus)

BREEDING RANGE: Southern Labrador west to
southern Alaska, south to northern Indiana and south
along coast to central California; California south to
western Mexico

WINTER RANGE: Breeding range south to Mexico
and east to Florida; withdraws from northernmost
portion of breeding range

PREFERRED HABITAT: Conifers, thickets

PREFERRED NEST SITE: Conifer

CLUTCH SIZE: 2 to 6, usually 3 or 4

INCUBATION PERIOD: 12 to 14 days

NESTLING PERIOD: 12 to 15 days

BROODS PER SEASON: 1

PREFERRED FOOD: Insects, buds, seeds

4½" L

5½" L

FRINGILLIDAE—
FINCHES

American Goldfinch
(Carduelis tristis)

BREEDING RANGE: Newfoundland west to British Columbia, south to southern California through Colorado to North Carolina

WINTER RANGE: Breeding range except northern portion to northern Mexico, Gulf states, and Florida

PREFERRED HABITAT: Fields, pastures, swamps

PREFERRED NEST SITE: Leafy bushes or trees

CLUTCH SIZE: 4 to 6, usually 5

INCUBATION PERIOD: 12 to 14 days

NESTLING PERIOD: 11 to 15 days

BROODS PER SEASON: 1 or 2

PREFERRED FOOD: Insects, buds, seeds

FRINGILLIDAE—
FINCHES

Red Crossbill
(Loxia curvirostra)

BREEDING RANGE: Newfoundland to northeastern Pennsylvania west to Alaska, south through the western mountains to Central America

WINTER RANGE: Permanent resident in breeding range; wanders south to the Gulf coast

PREFERRED HABITAT: Coniferous forests

PREFERRED NEST SITE: Conifer

CLUTCH SIZE: 3 to 5, usually 4

INCUBATION PERIOD: 12 to 14 days

NESTLING PERIOD: 15 to 17 days

BROODS PER SEASON: 1

PREFERRED FOOD: Seeds, especially of conifers, buds, wild fruits

BIBLIOGRAPHY

Armstrong, Edward A. *A Study of Bird Song.* London: Oxford University Press, 1963.

Audubon, John James. *The Bird Biographies of John James Audubon.* Ed. and selected by Alice Ford. New York: Macmillan, 1957.

———. *The Birds of America.* Intro. William Vogt. New York: Macmillan, 1937.

Baldwin, Ed, and Stevie Baldwin. *Building Birdhouses and Bird Feeders.* Garden City, NY: Doubleday, 1985. This book has only the most general of information about birds, speaking of finches or doves but not identifying them fully. The houses and feeders, many of them extremely complicated to make, are brightly colored and profusely ornamented, indicating that they are intended to please people, not birds.

Barbour, Roger W., Clell T. Peterson, Delbert West, Herbert E. Shadowen, and A. L. Whitt, Jr. *Kentucky Birds: A Finding Guide.* Lexington: University of Kentucky Press, 1973.

Bent, Arthur C. *Bent's Life Histories of North American Birds.* Ed. and abridged by Henry Hill Collins, Jr. 2 vols. New York: Harper & Brothers, 1960. This is a good way to introduce yourself to Bent's many volumes of bird histories. One volume covers land birds; the other covers water birds. It is chatty and informative.

———. *Life Histories of North American Blackbirds, Orioles, Tanagers, and Allies.* U.S. National Museum Bulletin 211. Washington, DC: GPO, 1958. This publication and the entries following are very valuable. They are detailed reports of what is known of specific birds, the information gathered from observers all over the country. Fascinating stuff—with plenty of blanks due to the difficulty of observing the private lives of birds. Don't let the word "bulletin" fool you; these are no pamphlets, but big thick books. The one on cardinals, etc., is 1,889 pages.

———. *Life Histories of North American Birds of Prey.* Part I. U.S. National Museum Bulletin 167. Washington, DC: GPO, 1937.

———. *Life Histories of North American Birds of Prey.* Part II. U.S. National Museum Bulletin 167. Washington, DC: GPO, 1938.

———. *Life Histories of North American Cardinals, Grosbeaks, Buntings, Towhees, Finches, Sparrows, and Allies.* Parts I, II, and III. U.S. National Museum Bulletin 237. Washington, DC: GPO, 1968.

———. *Life Histories of North American Cuckoos, Goatsuckers, Hummingbirds and Their Allies.* U.S. National Museum Bulletin 176. Washington, DC: GPO, 1940.

———. *Life Histories of North American Flycatchers, Larks, Swallows and Their Allies.* U.S. National Museum Bulletin 179. Washington, DC: GPO, 1942.

———. *Life Histories of North American Gallinaceous Birds.* U.S. National Museum Bulletin 162. Washington, DC: GPO, 1932.

———. *Life Histories of North American Jays, Crows, Titmice.* U.S. National Museum Bulletin 191. Parts I and II. Washington, DC: GPO, 1946.

———. *Life Histories of North American Nuthatches, Wrens, Thrashers and Their Allies.* U.S. National Museum Bulletin 195. Washington, DC: GPO, 1948.

———. *Life Histories of North American Thrushes, Kinglets, and Their Allies.* U.S. National Museum Bulletin 196. Washington, DC: GPO, 1949.

_____. *Life Histories of North American Wagtails, Shrikes, Vireos, and Their Allies.* U.S. National Museum Bulletin 197. Washington, DC: GPO, 1950.

_____. *Life Histories of North American Woodpeckers.* U.S. National Museum Bulletin 174. Washington, DC: GPO, 1939.

_____. *Life Histories of North American Wood Warblers.* Parts I and II. U.S. National Museum Bulletin 203. Washington, DC: GPO, 1953.

Berger, Andrew J. *Bird Study.* New York: Dover, 1961.

Birds of North America: A Guide to Field Identification. New York: Golden Press, 1966. This excellent guide gives notes on songs and migration routes as well as field identification marks. The nomenclature is outdated, however.

Burton, John A., and D. H. S. Risdon. *The Love of Birds.* London: Octopus, 1975. A coffee-table-type book with beautiful photographs of interesting and/or exotic birds of the world.

Cerny, Walter. *A Field Guide in Color to Birds.* Trans. Margot Schierlova. London: Cathay, 1975. This fascinating book, though it ignores completely many North American birds, gives the reader an idea of the distribution of different families, including some common in North America.

Choate, Ernest A. *The Dictionary of American Bird Names.* Boston: Gambit, 1973. Both common and scientific names are included, but the nomenclature is outdated.

Collins, Henry Hill, Jr. *Complete Field Guide to American Wildlife.* New York: Harper & Row, 1959.

_____, and Ned R. Boyajian. *Familiar Garden Birds of America.* New York: Harper & Row, 1965.

Cruickshank, Allan D., and Helen G. Cruickshank. *1001 Questions Answered About Birds.* New York: Dodd, Mead, 1958.

DeGraff, Richard M., Gretchin M. Witman, John W. Lanier, Barbara J. Hill, and James M. Keniston. *Forest Habitat for Birds of the Northeast.* Forest Service, USDA. Washington, DC: GPO, n.d.

Friedmann, Herbert. "Additional Data on the Host Relations of the Parasitic Cowbirds." Smithsonian Miscellaneous Collections. Vol. 149, #11. Washington, DC: GPO, 1966.

_____. *The Cowbirds: A Study in the Biology of Social Parasitism.* Springfield, IL: Charles C Thomas, 1929.

Green, Janet C., and Robert B. Janssen. *Minnesota Birds: Where, When, and How Many.* Minneapolis: University of Minnesota Press for the James Ford Bell Museum of Natural History, 1975. Among other features, this book has good photographs.

Griffin, Donald R. *Bird Migration: The Biology and Physics of Orientation Behavior.* Garden City, NY: Doubleday, 1964.

_____. *Bird Migration.* 2nd ed. New York: Dover, 1964.

Griscom, Ludlow. *Modern Bird Study.* Cambridge, MA: Harvard University Press, 1945.

Harrison, George H. *The Backyard Bird Watcher.* New York: Simon & Schuster, 1979. This book is excellent for the beginner, having all sorts of information on equipment, planting, cover, feeding, and water. It gives the National Wildlife Federation plan for the Backyard Wildlife Program and how to achieve success, showing examples in various states. The photographs are excellent.

Harrison, Hal H. *A Field Guide to Birds' Nests: Of 285 Species Found Breeding in the United States East of the Mississippi River.* Boston: Houghton Mifflin, 1975.

_____. *A Field Guide to Western Birds' Nests.* Boston: Houghton Mifflin, 1979.

Hartshorne, Charles. *Born to Sing: An Interpretation and World Survey of Bird Song.* Bloomington: Indiana University Press, 1973.

Headstrom, Richard. *Birds' Nests: A Field Guide: An Identification Manual to the Nests of Birds of the United States East of the One Hundredth Meridian.* New York: Ives Washburn, 1961. This illustrated book is a terrific field guide. It is well organized and full of information, with site, size, and materials used as the clues to identification.

Jewett, Stanley G., Walter P. Taylor, William T. Shaw, and John W. Aldrich. *Birds of Washington State.* Seattle: University of Washington Press, 1953. This book, published in cooperation with the U.S. Department of the Interior, Fish and Wildlife Service, is well done and informative. However, it lists as separate species many birds which seem to be only very slightly different. For example, it lists eight different song sparrows as species.

Kress, Stephen W. *The Audubon Society Guide to Attracting Birds.* New York: Charles Scribner's Sons, 1985. All you need to know, including how to plant nursery and wild stock and protect it from mice, rabbits, and deer, is in this guide. You'll learn how to select plants in various parts of the country and what weeds are attractive to birds, how to make pools and ponds, and what nurseries sell the plants suggested. An excellent annotated bibliography is appended.

Lambert, Terence. *Lambert's Birds of Garden and Woodland.* New York: Scribner's, 1976. Paintings by Terence Lambert, text by Alan Mitchell. This is an absolutely beautiful and charming book on British birds. Among them, of course, are the starling and house sparrow and many others that they call by different familiar names.

Lawrence, Louise de Kiriline. *The Lovely and the Wild.* New York: McGraw-Hill, 1968. This is an anecdotal book with charming illustrations by Glen Loates. It is chiefly useful to the person doing recreational reading about birds and what they can mean to the individual.

Leahy, Christopher. *The Birdwatcher's Companion: An Encyclopedic Handbook of North American Birdlife.* New York: Bonanza, 1984. This is an excellent reference book.

Lyttle, Richard B. *Birds of North America.* New York: W. H. Smith, 1983.

Mallett, Sandy. *A Year with New England Birds: A Guide to Twenty-Five Field Trips.* Somersworth: New Hampshire Publishing Company, 1978.

Mathews, F. Schuyler. *Field Guide of Wild Birds and Their Music.* Rev. ed. New York: G. P. Putnam's Sons, 1921. Considered a landmark in the study of bird song, this book has long been out of print but is widely available in public libraries. The original edition was published in 1904. The subtitle says it all: "A Description of the Character and Music of Birds, Intended to Assist in The Identification of Species Common in the United States East of the Rocky Mountains." Although mostly a discussion of bird song, it contains some interesting anecdotal material.

Mead, Chris. *Bird Migration.* New York: Facts on File Publications, 1983.

Miller, Alden H. "An Analysis of the Distribution of the Birds of California." *University of California Publications in Zoology.* Vol. 50, #6. Berkeley and Los Angeles: University of California Press, 1950-51.

Murton, R. K. *Man and Birds.* New York: Taplinger, 1972. This is mostly about British birds.

National Geographic Society. *Field Guide to the Birds of North America,* 2nd ed. Washington, DC: National Geographic Society, 1987.

Ornstein, Hollie A. "With 21 Million on the Prowl, Birding Becomes Big Business." *New York Times* News Service. *The Berkshire Eagle.* 26 March 1986.

Parry, Gareth, and Rory Putnam. *Birds of Prey*. New York: Simon & Schuster, 1979. A large coffee-table book, this was first published in England as *The Country Life Book of Birds of Prey*. It has beautiful plates.

Peterson, Roger Tory. *The Birds*. New York: Time, 1963.

_____. *A Field Guide to the Birds: A Completely New Guide to All the Birds of Eastern and Central North America*. 4th ed. Boston: Houghton Mifflin, 1980. A good field guide, but the nomenclature is outdated.

_____. *A Field Guide to the Birds: Giving Field Marks of All Species Found East of the Rockies*. 2nd rev. ed. Boston: Houghton Mifflin, 1947.

_____. *A Field Guide to Western Birds*. 2nd ed. Boston: Houghton Mifflin, 1961. Another good field guide with outdated nomenclature.

Pough, Richard H. *Audubon Western Bird Guide: Land, Water, and Game Birds*. Garden City, NY: Doubleday, 1957.

Proctor, Noble. *Garden Birds: How to Attract Birds to Your Garden*. Emmaus, PA: Rodale, 1986. Originally published in Great Britain in 1985, this book was adapted for the United States.

Rand, Austin L. *Ornithology: An Introduction*. New York: Norton, 1967.

Rubinfien, Elisabeth. "Police in Tokyo Stop Traffic to Make Way for Some Ducklings." *Wall Street Journal*. 11 June 1987.

Savage, Candace. *Wings of the North: A Gallery of Favorite Birds*. Minneapolis: University of Minnesota Press, 1985. This is a breathtakingly beautiful book.

Simon, Hilda. *The Courtship of Birds*. New York: Dodd, Mead, 1977. This book concerns itself primarily with spectacular and exotic birds: peafowl, birds of paradise, lyrebirds, black grouse, bower birds, penguins.

Simonds, Calvin. *Private Lives of Garden Birds*. Emmaus, PA: Rodale, 1984. This excellent, sensitively written book focuses on ethology, that specialty of behavioral science founded by Konrad Lorenz that looks at nature from the point of view of the organisms that live in it.

Stillwell, Norma. *Bird Songs: Adventures and Techniques in Recording the Songs of American Birds*. Garden City, NY: Doubleday, 1964. This is a folksy narrative, pleasant to read.

Stokes, Donald W. *A Guide to the Behavior of Common Birds*. 2 vols. Boston: Little, Brown, 1979.

Sutton, George Miksch. *Oklahoma Birds: Their Ecology and Distribution, with Comments on the Avifauna of the Southern Great Plains*. Norman: University of Oklahoma Press, 1967.

Taverner, P. A. *Birds of Eastern Canada*. Ottawa: F. A. Acland, 1922.

Thomas, Jack Ward, Robert O. Brush, and Richard M. DeGraaf. "Invite Wildlife to Your Backyard." Rev. reprint from *National Wildlife Magazine*. January 1987.

Tunnicliffe, C. F. *Sketches of Bird Life*. New York: Watson-Guptill, 1981. Tunnicliffe was a British artist (1901-1979) primarily of wildlife, although he also did domestic and farm animals. He became interested in birds and devoted much of his fifty-year career to drawing them. The book contains finished watercolors, field studies, and studio sketches based on field studies. It is fascinating, informative—and absolutely gorgeous. In it are courtship displays, distraction displays, nestlings, broods, birds in flight, studies of the bills of swans, and so on. The concentration, if any, is water birds, water being one of his specialties.

Weinert, Susan J., ed. *North American Wildlife*. Pleasantville, NY: Reader's Digest, 1982. Good for its purposes, this is a guide to 2,000 plants and animals. Although very general, it's rather fun.

INDEX

NOTE: When a page number appears in italics, an illustration or photograph appears on that page. A boldface numeral indicates that a description of the bird appears on that page.